EARLY AMERICAN MILLS

EARLY AMERICAN MILLS

by

MARTHA & MURRAY ZIMILES

 Bramhall House · New York

ACKNOWLEDGMENTS

We would like to give special thanks to the following people for unselfishly sharing with us their personal research and for giving us advice and encouragement:

Richard Candee, Curator of Architecture, Old Sturbridge Village; Randolph Langenbach; Donald Martin; Professor William Pierson of Williams College; Robert Vogel, Curator of Mechanical and Civil Engineering, Smithsonian Institution, Washington, D.C.

In each state we were helped in innumerable ways by individuals, businesses, historical societies, museums, and libraries. Without their help our task could never have been accomplished. We would therefore like to gratefully acknowledge the following individuals and organizations:

CONNECTICUT

American Thread Company, Willimantic; Antiquarian and Landmark Society, Inc., of Connecticut, Hartford; Bristol Clock Museum; Connecticut Historical Commission, Hartford; Connecticut League of Historical Societies, Inc.; Connecticut State Library, Hartford; Hitchcock Chair Company, Riverton; New London County Historical Society; Simsbury Public Library; Stowe-Day Foundation, Hartford; Seth Thomas Division of General Time Corporation, Thomaston; Mr. Robert S. Woodruff, New Preston.

MAINE

Aroostook Historical Society, Auburn; Bangor Historical Society; Biddeford Public Library; Greater Portland Landmarks, Inc.; Maine Department of Economic Development, Augusta; Maine Historical Society, Portland; Donald Martin, Wiscasset; Pejepscot Paper Division, Hearst Corporation, Brunswick; Society for the Preservation of Historic Landmarks, York County, York.

MASSACHUSETTS

American Optical Company, Southbridge; Berkshire County Historical Society, Pittsfield; Bernardston Historical Society; Commonwealth of Massachusetts Department of Commerce and Development, Boston; Connecticut Valley Historical Museum, Springfield; Crane Museum, Dalton, and Crane and Co., Inc., Mrs. Theodore Cronyn, Bernardston; Draper Division, North American Rockwell Corporation, Hopedale; Fall River Historical Society; Laurence Keeler of the Whitin family; Merrimack Valley Textile Museum, North Andover; National Park Service, Saugus; New Bedford Public Library; Noble and Cooley Company, Granville; Old Sturbridge Village; Sandwich Historical Society; Sheafe Satterthwaite, Williams College; Society for the Preservation of New England Antiquities, Boston; Whitinsville Machine Company.

NEW HAMPSHIRE

Herman Chase, Alstead; Claremont Public Library; Moody C. Dole; Manchester Historical Association; New Hampshire Historical Library, Concord; State of New Hampshire Department of Resources and Economic Development, Office of Industrial Development, Concord; Yankee Magazine, Inc., Dublin.

NEW YORK

Cohoes Industrial Terminal; Hudson River Valley Commission, Tarrytown; Landmark Society of Western New York, Rochester; Nassau County Historical Museum, Long Island; New York State Council on Architecture, New York; New York State Historic Trust, Albany; New York State Historical Association, Cooperstown; State of New York, Department of Parks and Recreation, Albany; University of the State of New York, State Education Department, Albany.

RHODE ISLAND

Allendale Public Library; Mrs. Edwin H. Arnold, Roaring Brook Farm, Greene; Louis Besettes, Manchoag; Carolina Public Library; Jamestown Historical Society; Old Slater Museum, Pawtucket; Providence Preservation Society; Providence Public Library; Rhode Island Development Council, Providence.

VERMONT

Barre Historical Society; Bellows Falls Historical Society; Atherton Bemis, Cavendish; A. S. Bennett, Jericho; Brooks Memorial Library, Brattleboro; Proctorsville Branch of the Fletcher Town Library; Shelburne Museum; State of Vermont Development Department, Montpelier; *The Weekly Reformer*, Brattleboro.

GENERAL

Eleutherian Mills Historical Library, Eleutherian Mills Hagley Foundation, Wilmington, Delaware; Historic American Buildings Survey, United States Department of the Interior, Washington, D.C.; Smithsonian Institution, Washington, D.C.

To Janet Y. Rogers
and
Pushkin

CONTENTS

INTRODUCTION

In writing this book on mills we have based our selection of buildings primarily on aesthetics. It is, therefore, a reflection of personal taste. We are well aware that other considerations play a part in a structure's ultimate worth and value, and we have tried to point up these social, economic, and historical factors. The northeastern states include a vast territory that has never before been systematically combed for mills and no doubt we have missed some worthy old buildings. Others may be conspicuous for their absence. Though of special historic interest, such mills are so lacking in aesthetic appeal that we preferred not to include them.

It is our hope that this book will be an excursion into a much ignored and neglected part of our architectural and engineering heritage. We have tried to gather a visual documentation of America's industrial beginnings. We have done this for various reasons. First, these relics and remains are quickly disappearing with no record at all. Barely a handful of early "domestic" mills survives in any authentic form, and our records for them are mostly of things of the past. Of the larger industrial mills, especially textile mills, many have been lost and a large number are in an alarming state of decay. We hope to sharpen the reader's vision and increase his awareness of the functional beauty of mills of all types. Second, we hope to overcome some of the prejudices against the later industrial mills, prejudices that stem from social concerns and blot out all others. On a surprising number of occasions we have been asked why we wish to preserve and admire buildings where severe oppression and exploitation of working people took place. Our reply is that unpleasant history is no excuse for the destruction of those monuments by which history is known. For better or for worse, the history of America cannot be told without a long look at industry. As with any institution, there were some benefits to balance the abuses. One of the things that surprised us while making this study is the way very early industry compares favorably with today's. It is doubtful whether a member of the modern assembly line has the pride and dignity of a Lowell operative in 1830.

It is our wish, then, to communicate some of our enthusiasm for old mills so that more people will see something worth saving in them and will do something about them.

In organizing our material we have tried to show the transition from local "domestic" and farm industries to the factory system of the nineteenth century. In our discussion of early mills the focus of attention has been as much upon how they work as how they were built. The two are inseparable. It is the ingenuity and the sheer beauty of the old waterwheels, windsails, and wooden gears that inspire admiration. There are bound to be technical parts that the less mechanically oriented of our readers will prefer not to ponder over.

In our discussion of textile mills we review first the social aspects that played such an important part in the architecture itself. Second, we devote a great deal of space to the development of industrial architecture in the cotton industry since it is here that the forms evolved that were later taken up by other industries. A third section is devoted to industrial buildings of interest that housed other industries. In the final section we discuss preservation and suggested uses for industrial buildings, giving examples of useful conversions.

We became interested in mills from our travels in New England. It seemed that everywhere we went these strange, usually empty buildings were to be found, but no one seemed able to tell us much about them. We were prompted to compile our picture collection and to investigate further into mills because of the desperate situation we found everywhere. Mills of all kinds are rapidly deteriorating through almost total neglect and disregard. All too frequently we would arrive at a town looking for a specific mill only to hear that it had burned, collapsed, or been torn down in the past year or two. Many a doctoral dissertation has been expounded on the tenth column or north frieze of the Parthenon, but here in our country a rich field of study is just waiting for the "experts." We decided not to wait for the experts since so many mills are disappearing. In all, we traveled about twenty-five thousand miles, wearing out one noble VW in the process. We hope our efforts will encourage others to investigate the subject and, more importantly, to see mills as worthwhile and useful buildings.

EARLY
AMERICAN
MILLS

1
EARLY MILLS

EARLY MILLS

FOR THE EARLY SETTLERS OF THE AMERICAN COLONIES THE immediate necessities of life were food, shelter, and clothing. In their European homelands the colonizers had been accustomed to seek the services of various kinds of mills to fill these needs. Water and wind-powered gristmills ground flour for life-sustaining bread and feed for animals. Sawmills supplied lumber for all kinds of building. Fulling mills worked woolen homespun into a wearable fabric, and iron furnaces supplied all-important metal for countless uses.

When European civilization burst upon America's stone-age population, there were no mills, dams, or furnaces.

Among the immigrants to the New World—the riff-raff, religious sectarians, and adventuresome aristocrats—were many people skilled in milling. They brought with them a technology that had evolved over centuries. Since the population of colonial America was small and labor in short supply most communities were anxious to attract men skilled in the technology of mill building to provide their citizens with worksaving machines.

Millers were granted free land and guaranteed water rights, and free labor was provided to help build many an early mill. Laws were passed eliminating competition, by providing that only one mill could be built within a given area, further ensuring a profitable enterprise.

These enticements did not go unnoticed. Mills were set up on the many

Davisons mill, East Rock-
away, New York, 1688.
Built by Joseph Haviland.
Destroyed.
Photo Courtesy Nassau
County Historical Museum

streams, brooks, and rivers that abounded, and villages formed around the mill. Countless place names reveal their mill-oriented beginnings. By 1880 mills were almost as plentiful as churches. The miller, millward, or millwright (a term that eventually designated only the mill builder) was a special man. He was accomplished in many areas: carpentry, architecture, engineering, basic mechanics, and hydraulics. Simple mechanical principles such as gearing, the lever, the inclined plane, the wedge, the screw, the pulley and cord, and the crank were all incorporated into the structure of the machinery of mills. This did not mean that a skilled Yankee carpenter could not pick up much of the information by studying existing mills. There were in circulation a number of books on millwrighting. The most famous, *The Young Millwright and Miller's Guide,* by the inventor Oliver Evans, appeared in 1795.

Mills were not only practical places of industry, they were also gathering places, much like the country store and post office. Almost every man at one time or another stopped at the mill to have his grain ground, his wood sawed, or some other task performed. Mills became centers of gossip and information. The miller was naturally the pivotal person around which this activity centered. This, in turn, led him into the position of adviser. Because his income came from many sources and everyone required his services, he prospered, taking pay in barter, money, or toll—a certain percentage of the milled grain. The amount was strictly regulated. Any miller caught overcharging was subject to stiff fines and even confiscation of his mill. The miller's prosperity led to other activities such as moneylending and trading. Given this accumulation of skills, wealth, and exposure to the populace, he easily became involved in politics. His importance was acknowledged by the town leaders who bestowed upon him the title of "master." Many a miller became a leader of the town council or even mayor.

Mills had more than a strictly utilitarian function. Most people who have visited a picturesque mill nestled along a river, stream, or millpond would find it a beautiful, if not romantic, place. Indeed, many a courtship flourished there. We are all familiar with the song "Down by the Old Mill Stream." At the other extreme, the expression "to go through the mill" refers to enduring great hardship and pain. The miller, while tending the great wheel that drove his machine, on occasion slipped in and was crushed. When millstones are found marking a grave, one would not be far wrong to assume that the stones were in use when such a misfortune occurred. Such stones were considered unlucky, and a graveyard was a fitting place to retire them.

WATERPOWERED MILLS

Whatever the water mill's use, its proper location was of the utmost importance. The river or stream to be used as power had to be examined throughout the year to determine whether there was a continuous flow of water. This was sometimes overlooked when no other site was available and the miller had to content himself with seasonal power. The best site was where little or no logging or land cultivation had taken place. Forests are natural umbrellas and windbreakers. They prevent the sun and wind from melting and evaporating rain and snow too quickly. The earth, old dried leaves, roots of trees, all act as sponges, soaking up the water and releasing it slowly. This ability to retain water prevents flashfloods after heavy downpours and dry streams after periods of drought.

Before setting up the mill, the miller had to determine the amount of head or fall that a stream could provide. Head refers to the distance water drops to the point of impact against the wheel: the percussion stage. Fall refers to the action of the water against the wheel below the point of impact: the gravity stage. It was difficult, for instance, to build a millpond on a river flowing along a perfectly flat tract of land. The miller had to accurately measure the quantity of water that flowed in a stream, for only by this method could he determine the amount of power available and hence the amount of work a stream could perform. He also had to check the irregularities in stream velocity and/or volume due to friction against the bed and banks; and, finally, he had to understand climatic changes in his locality since they, too, would affect the flow of water.

To ensure predictable water flow and to establish the head, dams were built. The dam created the millpond, which delivered the water steadily during the operation of the mill and replenished itself when the mill was idle. The storage capacity and head were determined by the size and height of the pond. Often, the aim was to provide enough water for one day's use of the regular mill function with enough extra to drive special machines.

The construction of the dam varied according to available materials and site. Where forests were plentiful, log dams were constructed. They were especially favored for tide mills as salt water had a corrosive effect on cemented rock dams. They had to be placed on secure foundations, be watertight, and attached securely to riverbanks, for the loss of the dam usually meant the destruction of the mill. Dams were often built more durably than mills, which can be seen from the numerous dams that are the sole mark of former mill sites. The most durable type of dam was made of large blocks of stone cut and fitted and joined with cement. Often built into the dams were fish ladders that permitted fish to climb the dam and spawn upstream.

The millrace, also called the penstock, was a ditch, trough, or pipe made of earth, wood, iron, or cement, which conveyed the water from the dam to a sluiceway that regulated the flow of water. In the later mills two racks were placed across the race to prevent debris from falling into the wheels. Logs, twigs, or even small stones could cause heavy damage to the wheel. The first rack was coarse, being designed to stop only large objects. It was followed by a fine rack that stopped smaller objects as well. They had to be kept clean to keep the flow and head constant so as not to impair the efficiency of the wheel.

Blow Me Downe mill, Plainfield, Vermont, c. 1820. The building was converted to a house; no equipment remains. The dam is in excellent condition. The mill is now deserted and should be restored.

Photo Courtesy of Authors

From the James Leffel catalog, c. 1880.
Photo Courtesy Merrimack Textile Museum

8

Gerritsen tide mill, Brooklyn, New York, 1636. Notice the rack made of wooden poles. Destroyed.

Photo Courtesy Nassau County Historical Museum

The sluiceway, mill run, flume, mill fleam, or mill way was the final passage through which the water flowed before reaching the wheel. It had a sluice gate, which opened and closed, controlling the amount of flow (see page 20).

The milltail, spillway, mill wash, wasteway, or tailrace was the water remaining after it had turned the wheel. This was sometimes returned to the stream or pond further down into another millrace to propel yet another wheel. A series of mills using common water often created major problems. If anything happened to the first mill—for example, if the dam broke—it usually meant damage, if not total destruction, to all the mills down the line. The expression "the old back's gone out" struck terror into numerous communities because it often meant that the grist, saw, fulling, and other mills were destroyed, bringing instantaneous destruction to the entire town's industries.

Other problems arose when the level of the stream fell. Water rights were carefully guarded. In fact, when one built or purchased a mill, water rights went with it. Even so, many a fight occurred over whether one mill was diverting more than its share of water.

Top and Bottom: Swedish mill, erected on Cobb's Creek, Philadelphia. This extremely old and primitive American mill was washed away by flood about 1927. Although a sluiceway is shown, the original mill operated as a Norse or Greek mill. The interior shows a ladder to the top of the hopper where grain is deposited. The shoe seems to have been vibrated by hand.

Photo Courtesy American Swedish Museum, Philadelphia

WATERWHEELS—HORIZONTAL WHEELS

The first use of water to supply power dates back to the first century B.C. The idea is believed to have originated in the Far East, either in China or India. The earliest type of water mill was used to grind grain and was a simple affair that required no gears. Here the runner stone (the top revolving millstone, the bottom one was stationary) was attached by a vertical shaft directly to a horizontal wheel and rotated at the speed of the wheel. The wheel was propelled by the force of the moving stream. This type of mill, having the simplest of all waterwheels, was called the Greek mill, and, in Scandinavia, the Norse mill. Although superseded by other types of wheels, the horizontal wheel was later to appear in modified form as the tub wheel and eventually as the turbine.

VERTICAL WATERWHEELS

The earliest form of a vertical wheel was formed by connecting two wagon wheels by a shaft. A series of slats were attached between the wheels. In some wheel types the slats were arranged to form buckets that would hold the water to use not only its force but its weight to rotate the wheel. These wooden wheels were vulnerable and needed constant attention. Although strong wood such as oak was used, it was reinforced with iron gudgeons, or iron sleeves that fit over a section of the shaft and side of the wheel. Eventually the wooden wheels were replaced by cast-iron ones.

OVERSHOT WHEELS

The overshot wheel was turned by the weight of water falling from above. It required a dam, the water being delivered by the millrace. The paddles were formed into buckets. A ten-foot wheel had about twenty-four buckets and a twenty-foot wheel had about fifty-six buckets. Overshot wheels were enormous, often reaching forty feet. The overshot was the most efficient of the three basic types of waterwheels. It reached up to 75 percent efficiency.

BREAST WHEELS

The breast wheel is so called because it receives water at its breast or center. Depending on whether the water hit above or below the wheel's axle, it was called a high breast or low breast wheel. The buckets on this wheel were close together and carried a smaller load of water than those of the overshot wheel. Its efficiency rate was about 65 percent.

A gristmill driven by a 22-foot diameter 3-foot face overshot waterwheel (C). (A) Man opening sluice gate. (B) 12-foot crown wheel attached to shafty waterwheel transmits the power to (E), a small bevel wheel on the upright shaft. A spur wheel (D) of 9 feet in diameter is placed on the upright shaft. This spur wheel works into the pinion (F) on the spindle, which drives the stone. The remaining gearing is used to drive other machinery. *Photo Courtesy Smithsonian Institution*

◄

Waterwheels: breast wheel (*left top and bottom*) and overshot wheel (*right top and bottom*). *Photo Courtesy New York Public Library*

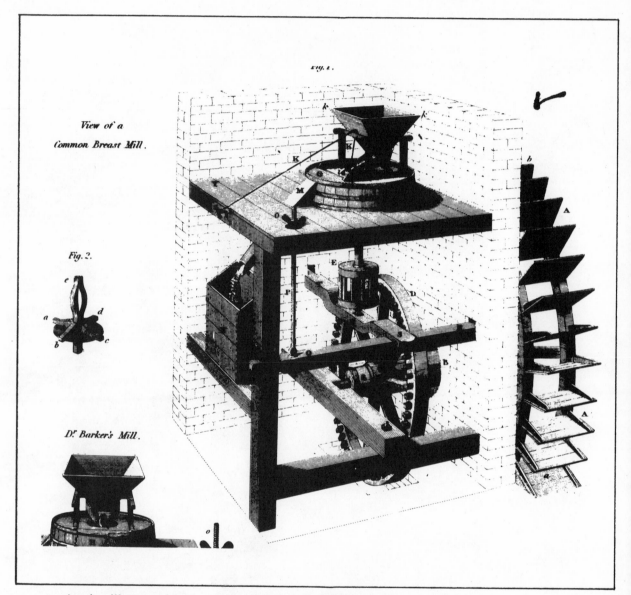

A gristmill powered by a common breast wheel. Although it is not shown, water hit the wheel above the axle. (A) Breast wheel, (a) bucket paddle, (B) wheel shaft, (D) face wheel, (E) lantern or wallower, (F) usually the place for an adjustable step bearing, but here it looks as if the entire apparatus rotated by (QR) was raised by turning wing bolt (O) (and another not seen), which in turn raised (S) and (F), thereby adjusting the distance between the runner and other stones. (G) Runner stone attached to the spindle and into (H), a vat or hoop. (L) Shoe feeding the grain through the eye of the runner. (M) A card attached to the runner sweeps the flour into a chute that deposits the flour into a hopper (N).   *Photo Courtesy Smithsonian Institution*

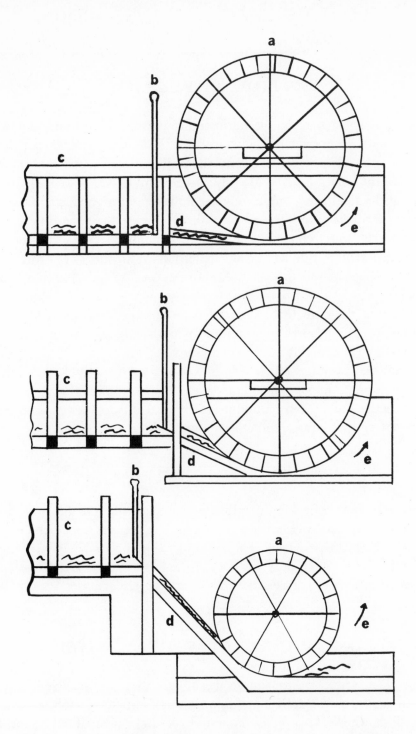

Three Types of
Undershot Wheels

a. Wheel
b. Sluice gate
c. Penstock
d. Sluiceway
e. Arrow indicates the
direction of rotation

This drawing was taken from
an illustration by Oliver Evans
in *Young Mill-Wright and
Miller's Guide* in the collection
of The Smithsonian Institution.

UNDERSHOT WHEELS

The undershot wheel was the least efficient, with a rate of about 30 percent, of the three major wheel types. It was often used in a running stream without a dam. If a dam was used, it had its sluice gate located so that water hit the bottom of the wheel. These wheels had many paddles; the greater the number the more energy created. The best formula for constructing such a wheel had the distance between the paddles equal to their width. Power, here, was generated by the speed and force of the flow.

TIDE WHEELS

The tide wheel may be placed in the category of the undershot wheel. It was usually smaller in size and had fewer paddles. It used the water from a tidal river or sea inlet. The water was controlled by two dams. One was in the usual place behind the wheel with a sluiceway and gate to deliver and release the water, the other at the tidal inlet where seawater flowed in at high tide and was trapped by the closing of the gate through which it had entered. As the tide receded, the dam next to the mill remained closed until enough water had receded to free the wheel that at high tide had been submerged. With the wheel free, the sluice gate could be opened and the seawater returned out the inlet after it had turned the wheel.

Sometimes the gate that admitted the seawater functioned automatically. A big stone, weighing up to five hundred pounds, was swung open as the water flowed in and swung slowly shut as the tide receded.

A great disadvantage of the tide mill was that the miller's schedule had to conform to the tidal movements. This, needless to say, made for a strange working day. Weather, too, often created problems: gales, northeasters, and occasional flood tides often did damage to both dam and mill.

PITCH-BACK WHEELS

The pitch-back wheel is so called because its rotation did not follow the usual clockwise direction. Here the water hit the buckets above the axle in the manner of a high breast wheel. The sluiceway, instead of being constructed out over the top of the wheel, only came up to the edge of it above the axle, causing the wheel to pitch back or revolve in toward the sluice gate. Its efficiency was comparable to that of the breast wheel.

FLOAT WHEELS OR PADDLE WHEELS

The float wheel was a simple affair, basically an undershot wheel that needed no dam or water delivery system. It was constructed with broad and long paddles. Two wheels were often mounted on either side of a boat or a single wheel was rigged between two pontoons or boats. The flow of a swift stream or river drove the wheels. The problem here was navigating the current, for often boats carrying valuable cargo capsized.

FLUTTER WHEELS

The flutter wheel was also an undershot wheel. It got its name from the fluttering sound the wheels made as the paddles cut through the water. Its shape was long and low like the wheel of an old paddle steamer. It was used where a

Saddle Rock tidewater gristmill, Great Neck, Long Island, New York, 1702, restored 1940–1955. Note the unusual roof line and facade with doors opening onto the river to receive grain from boats.   *Photo Courtesy Nassau County Historical Museum*

Tidewater mill, Huntington, Long Island, New York. West side of the harbor. Probably the Lefferts mill, c. 1793. Destroyed.
Photo Courtesy Nassau County Historical Museum

Roslyn gristmill, Roslyn, Long Island, New York. Note the enormous (about 20 feet) pitch-back wheel. Destroyed.
Photo Courtesy Nassau County Historical Museum

Perkins tidewater gristmill, Kennebunkport, Maine, 1749. Additions to the mill are used for a restaurant, but the mill building is intact. The cupola was added at a later date.
Photo Courtesy of Authors

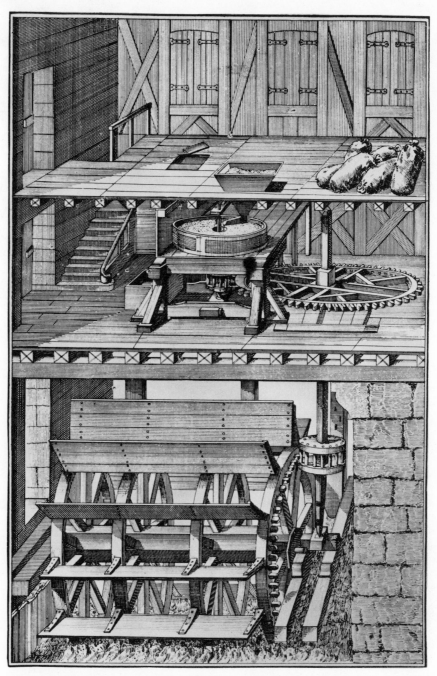

Gristmill, c. 1775, driven by a paddle wheel. Note the gear teeth on the side of the water-wheel eliminating the need for a face wheel.

Photo Courtesy
Smithsonian Institution

large supply of water with a head of six feet or more was available. Since the flutter wheel was small in diameter but powerful because of long paddles, it was possible, for example, to hook up a sawmill and provide one hundred revolutions per minute to the saw blade without complicated gearing. A typical wheel would have a three-foot diameter and six-foot-long paddles.

TUB WHEELS

The tub wheel, midway between a Greek wheel and turbine, was used when an eight-foot head could be obtained for the water supply. The tub wheel was horizontal and mounted in a bucket or tub, hence its name. The tub was con-

Carding mill built in South Waterford, Maine, c. 1835, moved to Old Sturbridge Village in 1963, and operated there by a tub wheel. Note the sluice gate and sluiceway in background.

Photo Courtesy of Authors

structed of wooden slats and reinforced with iron hoops. It was quite high, preventing water from shooting over it. The water entered the tubs at an angle through a sluice or metal tube and acted upon the wheel by percussion. The water filled the tub and descended to the wheel known as the runner, a vertical shaft having a series of blades emanating from its center. At first the runner was constructed of wood and eventually of iron, which in America came into use in the early 1800s. Much experimentation occurred with the tub wheel; in the first quarter of the nineteenth century the wheel was only 20 percent efficient; by 1830 it was closer to 40 percent; and ten years later experiments at Lowell, Massachusetts, and at the Franklin Institute in Philadelphia had produced a wheel that was 80 percent efficient.

EARLY AMERICAN MILLS

The tub wheel was the first to solve the icing problem. The water that fed the wheel was drawn from below the ice level of the stream, and since it constantly flowed into the tub freezing was not a problem. Millers had always struggled with that difficulty, trying everything from building wheels indoors to setting up heating systems, usually to no avail. Before the tub wheel, they were forced to close down and wait for spring.

TURBINES

The turbine is a modification of the tub wheel that greatly increases its power and efficiency. The Frenchman Fourneyron is credited with the invention of the first true turbine in 1827. He devised a system that fed water to the runner (horizontal wheel) through guide blades arranged around the outer rim of the runner and curved in the opposite direction from the runner's vanes. In this way water flowed through the machine in the opposite direction from the water in the tub wheel, thus creating a great force. The runner rotated a shaft to which the machinery was geared. The turbine was usually enclosed in a casing of cast iron so that a great amount of pressure was created by the water within. The water was delivered down a vertical pipe or shoot called the penstock (here the term includes the sluiceway), which was made of either wood, cast iron, or steel.

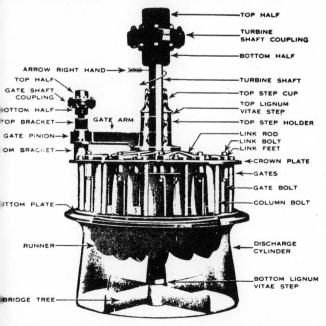

THE JAMES LEFFEL & CO

Improved Vertical Samson Turbines

These turbines are built strong and substantial, and equipped with our exclusive design double steel bucket runners fitted on steel shafts. Large top and bottom lignumvitae step bearings for carrying the revolving parts of these turbines, including the weight of extra upright shafting and gearing. Also, balanced swing-type gates with separate adjustable steel connections. Each removable independently. All bearings of large dimensions and special material. Bolted couplings.

TOP HALF
TURBINE SHAFT COUPLING
BOTTOM HALF
ARROW RIGHT HAND
TOP HALF
GATE SHAFT COUPLING
BOTTOM HALF
TOP BRACKET
GATE ARM
GATE PINION
BOTTOM BRACKET
TURBINE SHAFT
TOP STEP CUP
TOP LIGNUM VITAE STEP
TOP STEP HOLDER
LINK ROD
LINK BOLT
LINK FEET
CROWN PLATE
GATES
GATE BOLT
COLUMN BOLT
BOTTOM PLATE
RUNNER
DISCHARGE CYLINDER
BOTTOM LIGNUM VITAE STEP
BRIDGE TREE

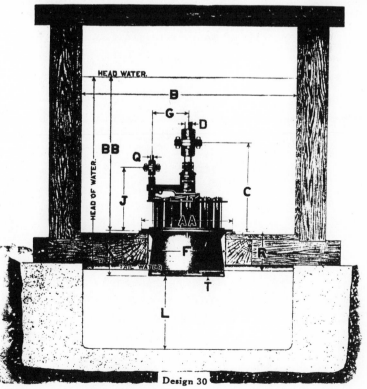

THE JAMES LEFFEL & CO

HEAD WATER.
B
G
D
BB
Q
HEAD OF WATER.
J
C
AA
F
TAIL WATER
R
T
L
Design 30

SPRINGFIELD, OHIO. U.S.A.

ESTABLISHED 1862

A number of old turbines at the East Vassalboro sawmill, Maine. See p. 56 for view of the mill.
Photo Courtesy of Authors

The problem of freezing did not arise since the water could flow into the penstock from beneath the ice that formed only on the surface of the pond or river. The turbine itself was installed at a level above the stream bed so that it would not be flooded by the tailrace. It was eventually found that if turbines were freely discharged into the atmosphere through open pipes, the proportion of head represented by the height above the tailrace would be lost. To solve this problem a draft tube was attached to the turbine. The water was discharged through this tube, which had its outlet submerged. This created a pressurized head.

Experimentation brought about several classifications of turbines, but Fourneyron's basic machine was so effective that it remained in use until replaced by steam or electric power. Turbines of all sizes were used to power everything from a single set of stones in a gristmill to the vast complexes of machinery in textile cities. They replaced the picturesque waterwheel because they were less susceptible to freezing and eliminated the costly reconstruction and endless repair of the wooden wheel. They also used less space and simpler gearing (such as rope and belt drive) to create more power with greater efficiency from the same head of water. The water was discharged from a turbine with great force. In big textile complexes, rather than waste this energy, the discharged water was channeled from the draft tube into another body of water such as a canal to create pressure for another head of water to power another turbine. Rather sophisticated engineering was needed to utilize the mighty rivers, networks of canals, to power the large mills.

Left: J. L. Dunnell & Son feed mill, Bernardston, Massachusetts, c. 1899. Rope drive coming off of turbine. *Photo Courtesy of Authors*

Lower left: Rope drive power system spanning distance of 100 feet. *Photo Courtesy of Authors*

Below: Rope drive entering feed mill. Note chute in foreground. *Photo Courtesy of Authors*

23

Gristmill powered by a turbine. Note wooden penstock and the belts driving stone spindles and grain elevators. Illustration from Poole & Hunt catalog, c. 1900.

Photo Courtesy Smithsonian Institution

GRISTMILLS

"No man shall take the nether or the upper millstone to pledge: for he taketh a man's life to pledge."

DEUTERONOMY 24:6

In the beginning it was human strength that ground grain, at first no more than a man's teeth. Then man probably took up two stones and rubbed the husks away with a simple grinding action. A mortar and pestle effect was also attempted, either with a hollow tree trunk and tree joint or with the laborsaving device of the sapling and stump mill where the pounding tool was raised by the spring action of the sapling. A primitive attempt to harness waterpower resulted in the plumping mill.

A return to stone grinding came with the introduction of the simple stone quern or first true millstone. It consisted of a stationary stone and a top or runner stone that was rotated by hand. The stone quern evolved into the rotary quern mill. For some strange reason this did not take place until a few hundred years ago.

The rotary grinding mill was further simplified by hitching animals to a millstone.

The use of animal power became more efficient with the treadmill, which was often geared to perform a number of functions.

It must be noted that although many of these primitive grinding methods were used centuries ago in Europe, they were all used in early America.

GRAIN

Before corn, wheat, or other grains could be taken to the mill, the grain had to be removed from the husk. In the case of corn, this was done by scraping the ear against a sharp knife whose blade was embedded in a table or other rigid surface. In several gristmills we have seen a corn sheller, a hand-cranked machine consisting of two pieces of rotating board studded with many iron points or nails. When an ear of corn was placed between them the rotating nailheads shelled the corn. Wheat had to be threshed. In the early days this was done by throwing the wheat into the air, allowing the wind to blow the chaff away, leaving the grain. Other methods involved beating the grain or treading upon it.

THE WATERPOWERED GRISTMILL

It is difficult to say exactly where and when the first gristmills were built in America. Devices for grinding grain were among the most immediate necessities of the earliest settlers. They probably used the primitive methods discussed

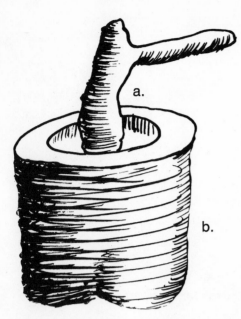

Hollow Tree Trunk and Tree Joint

a. Tree joint
b. Hollow tree trunk

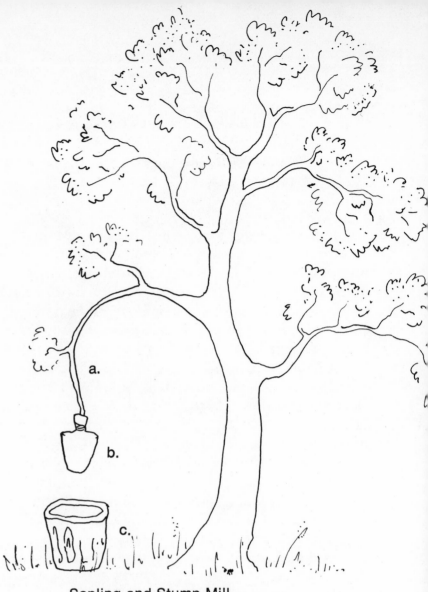

Sapling and Stump Mill

a. Spring action of sapling moves pounder
b. Pounder attached to sapling
c. Hollow tree trunk

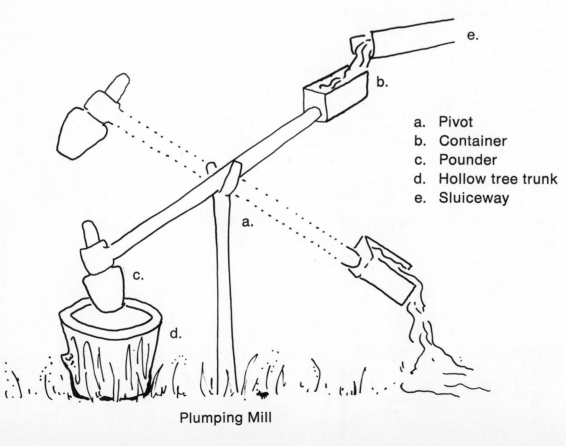

a. Pivot
b. Container
c. Pounder
d. Hollow tree trunk
e. Sluiceway

Plumping Mill

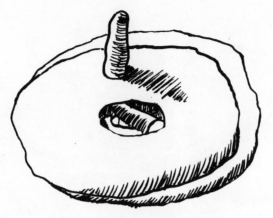

Stone Quern

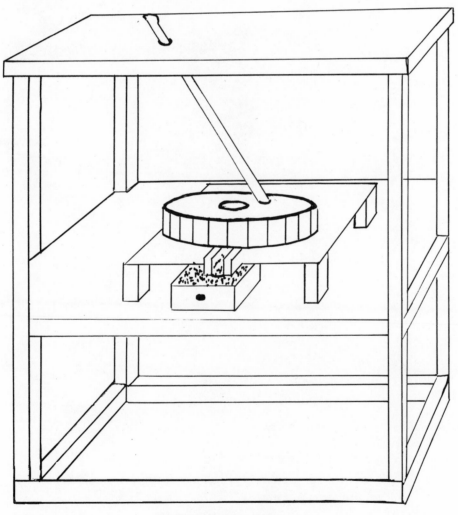

Rotary Quern Mill

Corn sheller located in Jamestown, Rhode Island. See color
photo facing page 51 for this
grist mill.
Photo Courtesy of Authors

until the more established settlements could build true gristmills. Some of the earliest known mills are included in the following list, which is by no means complete.

Massachusetts

WATERTOWN	1631
PLYMOUTH	1633
IPSWICH	1635
ROXBURY (tide mill)	1650
DORCHESTER	1663

Connecticut

STRATFORD	1639
NEW LONDON	1650–53

New York

NEW AMSTERDAM	1626

(with the possibility that a windmill was constructed immediately after)

BROOKLYN (Gerritsen tide mill)	1636

Gristmill powered by overshot wheel in New London, Connecticut. Originally built in 1650–
1653, it has been restored a number of times.   *Photo Courtesy of Authors*

MILLSTONES

In order to grind the grist, a pair of millstones were needed. At first, the stones were quarried locally. To this day one can hear a Rhode Islander talk about the superiority of his johnnycakes because they are made of cornmeal ground with stones made from Rhode Island granite. Other stones were made from quartz-shot sandstone. Sandstone of Ulster County, New York, and Lancaster County, Pennsylvania, was considered excellent, but French buhrstone was considered the best material for millstones. It was exported to America, not as whole millstones, but in pieces that were fitted and cemented together, then bound with iron hoops and backed with plaster. Stones varied in size, the average being four feet in diameter. Some were up to six feet wide and weighed more than a ton.

FURROWS

Both the upper stone, called the runner, and the lower stone, called the bed stone or nether, had to be furrowed. Furrows were a pattern of cuts on the bottom of the runner and on the top of the nether. The area left uncut between the furrows was called the land. Millers often would get into arguments on whose stones ground the best. The early patterns were sickle-shaped. Later ones were made with a variety of straight-line designs.

The furrows' function was threefold. First, the edges of the opposing furrows functioned like the blades of a pair of shears, ripping off the grain's outer husk. Second, the furrows acted to channel the ground flour to the edge of the stone. Finally, they admitted enough air to pass through the stones so as to carry out the heat generated by friction during the grinding. The land or flat areas did the actual grinding of the kernel into flour.

Although most mills had but one pair of stones, a few had more. Farmers would decide which stone was the best and would be sure to bring their grain on the day that stone was being used.

The man who cut the furrows was known as the millstone picker. His tool was the mill pick, or bill. At first, bills were made of iron, which tended to dull and chip easily. The tip was eventually replaced by steel.

It was important to keep the stones sharp since dull ones ground coarse,

◄

Sickle-furrowed millstones, (a) nether stone, (b) runner stone. Straight-line furrows, (c) nether stone.
Photos Courtesy of Authors

cakey flour, preventing bolting (the sifting of flour into grades of fineness) and hastening fermentation.

Built above the grinding area were a crane, grappling hooks, and screw hoist. The grappling hooks were inserted into two holes in the runner stone (see p. 78). The screw and crane hoist lifted the stone, swung it around, turned it over, and set it on the floor where recutting and sharpening took place. The bottom stone could be worked on in place. After a number of years the bottom stone wore down and had to be raised. This was done by a series of wedges hammered under the stone.

Each stone had a hole cut through its center. The hole in the runner was called the eye. In addition, the runner stone had two or four out cuts or notches on the hole. Through these holes passed the revolving shaft called the spindle. To the end of the spindle, which passed through the bed stone, was attached a mace-head. This was a device to which was attached the iron rynd or that piece which fitted into the notched hole of the runner stone. This created a situation whereby the spindle, geared to the waterwheel, passed up through the bed stone and notched into the runner stone to turn it. Distances between the two stones could be minutely adjusted by a step bearing at the base of the spindle. Distances of different degrees were used for each type of grain. The stones had to be perfectly balanced, both dynamically and statically. If the stones touched during grinding, the grain would be ruined and so would the precious stones. Worst of all was the danger of a spark igniting the mill. Flour dust was everywhere. Being of organic matter, it was highly flammable, and a single spark could cause an explosion.

The grain was poured into the hopper, a four-sided, tapering wooden chute placed above and to the side of the eye of the runner. The grain fell through the hopper into a narrow wooden trough or shoe, which hung loosely over the eye so that it could be gently tapped or vibrated to feed the grain to the stones in a slow steady flow. A small forked instrument called the damsel was attached to the rind so that it projected from the eye and rotated, hitting the shoe. The sounds made during this operation were referred to as the "song of the damsel." A string adjusted the angle of the shoe and the flow of the grain.

The millstones were enclosed in a wooden box called the vat or hoop. Construction of the vat varied, but it usually consisted of a series of vertical boards bound together around the stones with iron bands. A space of four to eight inches remained between the vat and the stone's edges. The vat covered the stones except for an opening in the top where the damsel protruded to tap the shoe.

Surrounding the bottom of the bed stone was a flat board that created a smooth space between the rim of the stones and the wall of the vat. Into this area fell the flour as it was ground and channeled out the furrows of the stones. A card or scoop attached to the runner scraped the flour along until it fell through a single hole and into a sack or bin below. Spillover grain was scooped up with wooden shovels to avoid sparks.

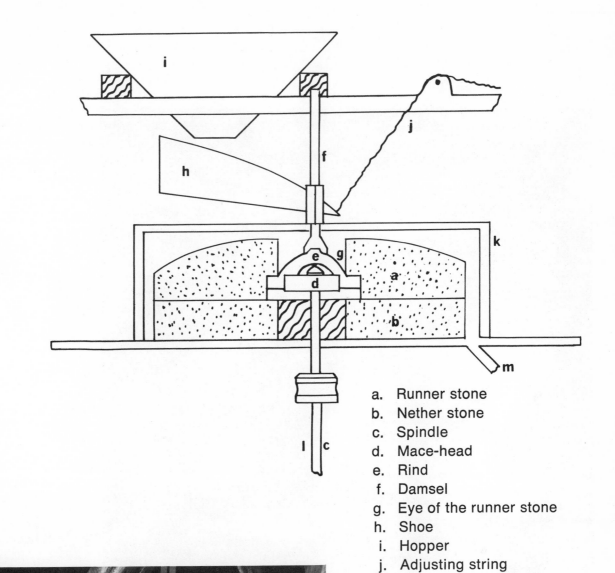

a. Runner stone
b. Nether stone
c. Spindle
d. Mace-head
e. Rind
f. Damsel
g. Eye of the runner stone
h. Shoe
i. Hopper
j. Adjusting string
k. Vat
l. Spindle
m. Flour chute

Interior of Saddle Rock gristmill showing chute hopper, shoe grappling hooks, and wooden stone casing. For exterior see p. 17.
Photo Courtesy Nassau Historical Museum

Interior of the Wright gristmill, Old Sturbridge Village,
Massachusetts. Grinding floor
showing grain chute, vat, hopper, and shoe. Stones and hopper
are from the Porter gristmill,
Hebron, Connecticut.

Photo Courtesy of Authors

EARLY AMERICAN MILLS

Above: J. L. Dunnell & Son feed mill, Bernardston, Massachusetts, c. 1899. Note the hopper and grinding machine. A grain elevator deposits the grain in the machine.
Photo Courtesy of Authors

Left: Notice the hopper and grain elevators. The metal shovel hung on the post could prove dangerous; a wooden one should have been used.
Photo Courtesy of Authors

GEARING

The average waterwheel revolved slowly, usually about fifteen times a minute. Most millstones of forty-eight-inch diameter needed speeds of about 125 rpm. This was accomplished by gearing (see pages 14 , 77). Gears at first were constructed of hardwood, most often oak. The individual wooden teeth were replaceable. When one wore out, all that was necessary was to carve a new one and wedge it in. Later, in the first quarter of the nineteenth century, wooden gears were replaced by cast-iron ones.

In the typical early gristmill using any one of the vertical wheels, the waterwheel was paralleled by another large wheel attached to the same shaft. This wheel was called a face wheel. It meshed with a much smaller gear called the lantern gear or wallower, which turned a vertical shaft (see pages 77 , 98). The meshing of these two gears translated the vertical power of the waterwheel into the horizontal action needed for stones. In more primitive mills, the vertical shaft turned by the wallower went directly to the stones to turn the runner. This simple gearing is rarely found in America. More commonly the upper end of the vertical shaft turned a large horizontal wheel called the spur. It meshed with one or more lantern gears, which turned the spindles of one or more stones.

The various operations of milling were fitted into buildings with several stories. The typical gristmill was invariably arranged in vertical fashion. At the top floor were sacks of unprocessed grains, which were hoisted directly from the delivery wagon. From the top floor grain could be poured into the hopper and stones on the floor below. At the very bottom were gears and shafts. The wheel was usually out of doors, but sometimes the mill was built directly over the sluice with the wheel inside. With such an arrangement it was usual to have several laborers hoisting, shoveling grain, carrying sacks, and so on.

This was all changed by one of the early industrial revolution's inventive geniuses, Oliver Evans, who was born in Newport, Delaware, in 1755. As a young man he was apprenticed to a wheelwright. He was continually experimenting with laborsaving devices such as the steam engine and new uses for gears. His greatest accomplishment was the automatic flour mill. It used a system of elevators and descenders to move grain through the several stories of the mill. He also devised a system of horizontal movers based on the Archimedean screw, an endless metal screw, and an octagonal shaft with small paddles that spiraled the grain along on the horizontal plane. Another exceedingly original improvement was the hopper boy, a revolving rake and spreader used to dry and cool the flour. His genius was acknowledged by George Washington and Thomas Jefferson who both commissioned him to build gristmills.

The last stage of the milling process was bolting or sifting of flour into grades. The bolting machine invented by Evans consisted of a long rectilinear frame holding a long revolving hoop. The hoop was slightly tilted. It was covered with four fabrics or screens of varying weave. At the end where the flour was

Wooden shovel used to prevent sparking. Housed in Saddle Rock tidewater gristmill, Great Neck, Long Island, New York.

Photo Courtesy of Authors

Gristmill, c. 1870, and most likely sawmill, as can be seen from log in foreground. Location unknown. This is one of the few gristmills that has a clerestory monitor. Notice the sack hoist raising grain from the wagon.

Photo Courtesy Smithsonian Institution. Tintype from the collection of Robert M. Vogel,
curator of Mechanical and Civil Engineering

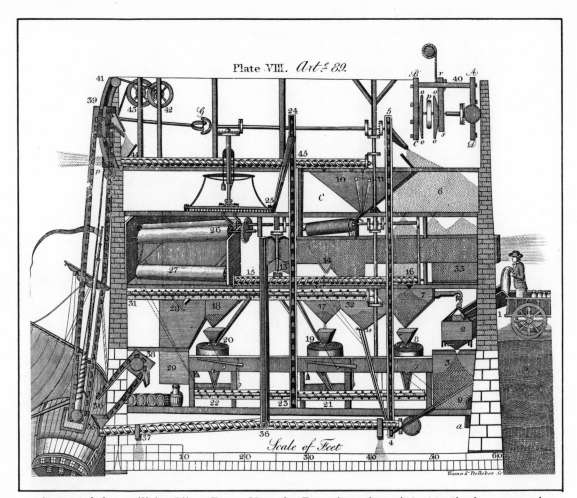

Automated flour mill by Oliver Evans. Note the Evans inventions: (39, 24, 5) elevators; grain descending by its own weight (e.g. 6); horizontal movers (31, 45, 37, 15); hopper boy (25). This diagram is from the 1834 edition of *The Young Millwright and Miller's Guide*.

Photo Courtesy Smithsonian Institution

introduced, a fine fabric sifted only the powdery flour. At the other end was the coarse weave that sorted the bran. Sacks were set under each "grade" to collect the flour. The finest was the most expensive and the most in demand. The second bag held the leftovers of the first. The third held middlings and the fourth held the shorts, considered the dregs of the flour. All grains were originally called flour after grinding, but eventually it was mainly wheat that came to be designated by that name.

In the early days flour mill came to mean a mill whose stones were well enough balanced to grind wheat, a process that required a minute space between the stones. Coarsely ground grain was called meal and was mixed with other ingredients to be used as animal feed.

Stone-ground flour was highly nutritious. Flour today is ground in high-speed rollers capable of producing flour a hundred times faster than a stone mill. In order to do this, an oily substance that chokes the rollers has to be removed. The substance, called the germ of the wheat, is sifted out in a preliminary process. Flour companies discovered a surprise advantage in their germless flour: it had a very long shelf life. The germ of the wheat is the part containing the vitamin and protein rich oil. To remove it is to take the life out of the flour, leaving little but useless starch.

Stone-ground grain is not only more nutritious, it is infinitely more flavorful. Many an old-time Yankee recipe will fail if old-time wisdom is not respected. One cookbook states it well:

> Much of our national illness is caused by crazes for food that is (1) white, (2) refined, (3) keepable. All three crazes are exemplified in white flour. The best food chemists are the earth and the sun, which produce the whole-wheat that the steel rollers of the white flour millers spoil. White flour makes white faces . . . food is stuff to be eaten fresh, not to be "kept" as if it were an heirloom . . . wholemeal flour naturally does not "keep" because the germ in it is alive. Germless white flour "keeps" because it is dead, because it is as dead as Portland cement powder, all its original goodness having been sifted out of it. Let them "keep" their flour who have no care to keep their health.*

THE GRISTMILL BUILDING

The mill structure that housed the stones, gears, and sacks of grain was exceedingly functional. In all the mills we visited, as well as those in the hundreds of photographs we leafed through, we found no ornament with the exception of a weather vane or sign. The usual architecture is most akin to barn construction. Almost all small mills had single-gabled roofs. Of the mills still standing, we know of only one, on Cape Cod, with a hip roof. Of the larger gristmills, most were of the simple gabled type, although a few gambrel-roofed mills were built. Rarer still are the gristmills that adopted the clerestory monitor so prevalent in textile mills of the first half of the nineteenth century. Also rare are those mills constructed with brick and stone, or in combination with wood.

As the gristmill evolved in the early days, a number of distinguishing features became part of the building. The ridge of the roof extended out toward the road so a hoist could be attached to raise the grain to the top floor from delivery wagons. One facade usually had a series of doors that opened on each floor to allow new equipment and/or tools to be hoisted. The other facades had

---

*Ellen and Vrest Orton, *Cooking with Whole Grains*. Farrar, Straus & Giroux, Inc., New York: 1951, p. 8.

double-hung windows for light and ventilation. Often the facade facing the wheel had fewer windows. This shielded the mill from the cold winds sweeping off the water and cut down on some of the noise of the wheel. On rare occasions dormer windows were installed to light the top floor.

Special features appeared in some circumstances. Some mills sprouted cupolas, perhaps so the miller could see the level of the sea or stream.

Exteriors were covered in either clapboard or shingles. The walls were constructed of braced frames characterized by heavy timber posts at the corners, often with intermediate posts between them. The whole structure rose from a heavy foundation sill to a heavy plate at the roof line. Enormous timber girts ran from post to post. All parts were joined by mortise joints. This consisted of mortising or cutting a slot in one member and forming a corresponding tenon or tongue in another. When they were assembled the tenon was held in place by a treenail or wooden peg inserted in a hole drilled through both members. Most of the beams were hand hewn. Often they were massive, spanning at times eighteen feet. They were usually of oak, a wood that termites do not care for. Today, as craftsmanship is dying out and we hurry to keep up with our time saving machines, the gristmill stirs our admiration for its careful, skillful workmanship and nostalgia for the days when men took the time to mortise joints and fashion the great wooden pegs.

A strong construction was needed to withstand the elements and the constant vibration of the wheel and stones. Even the best balanced stones would vibrate. To further strengthen the buildings, flood abutments were placed upstream or against the mill. The center of gravity of the mill rested over the center of the foundation, and the entire building rested on a deep foundation dug below the frost line.

The interiors were woody, stark, and arranged for functional tasks. Some mills had a series of trap doors for hoisting sacks and materials through the floor. The buildings must have been cold, for fireplaces were rare. The fear of burning down the mill was greater than the need for comfort. At most, a Franklin stove was permitted in the office. What really gave the mill its character was the machinery, most of all the wheel.

Yet, with all its beauty, the mill had its problems. Birds, rats, and mice infested every mill. If covered storage facilities were not available, the miller was forever having his handwoven gunnysacks eaten through. Flour dust was everywhere, creating both fire and health hazards. Millers were known for having lung trouble. Yet some millers of old seemed to have enjoyed their lot as a stanza from the song by Isaac Bickerstaff goes:

> I live by my mill, she is to me
> Like parent, child and wife
> I would not change my station
> For any other in life.

Stony Brook gristmill, West Brewster, Cape Cod, Massachusetts.   *Photo Courtesy of Authors*

Town gristmill, Hampton, New Hampshire.
Photo Courtesy of Authors

Wright gristmill, Old Sturbridge Village,
Massachusetts. A beautiful small gabled mill.
Photo Courtesy of Authors

Stony Brook gristmill, Stony Brook, Long Island, New York, c. 1750. The mill equipment remains intact and is powered by the overshot wheel. The simple gabled building has one dormer window.

Photo Courtesy of Authors

Old gristmill, North Kingston, Rhode Island, 1750, on the property of Gilbert Stuart and adjacent to the snuff mill. Formerly powered by a waterwheel, it was converted to a turbine. The remains of the turbine are still there. Note the old millstones used as steps into the mill. The interior still contains operable stones, hopper, shoe vat, and grappling hook. The building has a simple gabled roof. *Photo Courtesy of Authors*

Mill on Watts Pond, Valley Stream, Long Island, New York. Note the tiny dormer set into the gabled roof.

Photo Courtesy Nassau County
Historical Museum

Above: Thomas Chickering mill, Barnerville, New York, c. 1816. Much of the original equipment remains.

Photo Courtesy of Authors

Baxter mill, West Yarmouth, Massachusetts, 1789. This hip-roofed mill was converted to turbine power in 1840. When we visited the mill it was closed, hence the white shutters over the windows.

Photo Courtesy of Authors

Cog mill, Port Washington, Long Island, New York. Note the two waterwheels and gambrel roof.
Photo Courtesy Nassau County Historical Museum

Roslyn gristmill, Roslyn, Long Island, New York. A dispute has arisen as to the dating of the original mill. A mill was built in 1701 by John Robeson. Later Jeremiah Williams either added or rebuilt the present mill. This occurred between 1713 and 1741. It was acquired by Henry Onderdonk, the same man who owned the paper mill in Roslyn. The mill was restored in 1916 and is now used as a teahouse. It still has some original equipment. Notice the hoist used to raise grain. In the near future it may be restored to its original state and used as a historical museum.

Photo Courtesy Nassau County Historical Museum

Photo Courtesy of Authors

Chase's mill, East Alstead, New Hampshire, c. 1880. Powered by a turbine, this lovely mill still uses waterpower to run woodworking machines. Formerly a gristmill. *Photo Courtesy of Authors*

▼

Red mill, or Claverack mill, Claverack, New York. Built in 1767 on Claverack Creek by General Jacob R. Van Rensselaer. Originally ground grain and plaster. Most of the machinery has been removed, and it is now used as an antiques store. Note the grain hoist and double-hung windows. Front view.

Photo Courtesy of Authors

Plandome mill, Manhasset, Long Island, New York. Note the cupola. Destroyed.
Photo Courtesy Nassau County Historical Museum

Jericho gristmill, Jericho, Vermont, 1846. This mill had an overshot wheel. It is now used as a craft shop. Note the huge cupola and the use of stone and wood for the mill construction.

Photo Courtesy of Authors

Gristmill, Cold Spring Harbor, Long Island, New York. Probably the Hewlett, Jones and Company mill, 1791. The overshot wheel was placed so low that tides silted it up. The mill stood on a site that has housed mills since 1680. Note the shingles and few windows on the wheel facade.

Photo Courtesy Nassau County Historical Museum

Right: Isaac Satterly gristmill, located in Frank Melville Memorial Park, Setauket, Long Island, New York, c. 1824. A very unusual stone mill; most mills on Long Island were of wood.

Photo Courtesy Nassau County Historical Museum

Unidentified gristmill. A beautiful example of a fieldstone and wood mill. Note the waterwheel in ruins.   *Photo Courtesy Smithsonian Institution*

J. L. Dunnell & Son feed mill, Bernardston, Massachusetts, c. 1899. The only large commercially operating waterpowered mill that we saw. It is run by a turbine and rope drive system that spans a distance of over 100 feet. See also pp. 23, 35.

Photo Courtesy of Authors

Thomas Chickering mill, Barnersville, New York, c. 1818. Much of the original equipment remains.
Photo Courtesy of Authors

Red Mill, or Claverack mill, Claverack, New York. **Rear view.**

Photo Courtesy of Authors

Jamestown gristmill, Jamestown, Rhode Island, 1787. A smock windmill using a winch to turn its dome cap into the wind.

Photo Courtesy of Authors

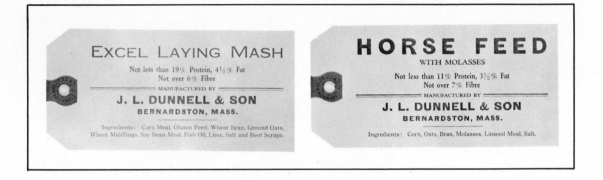
SAWMILLS

Sawmills were built as early as gristmills. In colonial America there were millions of acres of untouched forests. Wood was there for the taking; in fact, it was too plentiful. Many forests of huge first growth trees were simply burned off to make way for pasture and farmland. No community could be called self-sufficient without, at least, one sawmill. Gristmills and sawmills were often housed in the same structure or built close to one another, usually on the opposite banks of the same dam. In forest areas sawmills were built on available streams and rivers, which were also used to transport logs and boards to and from the mill.

Many of our early settlers were trained sawyers who sawed logs in pits called sawpits. There the top man, called the top sawyer, pulled up on the saw and guided it along a chalked line. The man in the pit, called the pitman, pulled down. (The surnames Sawyer and Pitman are derived from these occupations.) Logs were held in place by spikes and the men moved the saw against the log. Needless to say this wasn't a very efficient system. Even the most skilled could cut only between one hundred and two hundred board feet a day.

Tullers gristmill, Simsbury, Connecticut, 1688. Note the large overhang—a hoist raised grain from wagons below.

Photo Courtesy of Authors

Grist and sawmill, Pine Plains, New York. The sawmill is destroyed, but the gristmill, seen from the road, remains with much of its equipment. The Patchen homestead is in the background.
Photo Courtesy of Patchen Family

Old sawmill at the Patchen farm, Pine Plains, New York. Destroyed. *Photo Courtesy of Authors*

The Little River mill on the Little River in East Lebanon, Maine, is a combination mill consisting of a gristmill and shingle-clapboard mill. It was built by Joseph Hardison in 1774. He used hand-hewn timbers measuring up to 13 by 13 inches and spanning 22 feet without posts. The mill rests on 5-foot-thick dry-laid stone. Before it stopped operating, it was powered by a turbine. It is presently owned and being restored to its original use by Philip Johnson.

Photos Courtesy of Authors

Grist and sawmill, Cavendish, Vermont, 1860, run by Atherton Bemis as a sawmill only. It no longer uses waterpower. It was built by Mr. Bemis's grandfather. *Photo Courtesy of Authors*

EARLY AMERICAN MILLS

Top and Bottom: Harvey's mills, South Lee, New Hampshire, 1725. Combination grist- and sawmill. Some of the equipment remains. At some date it was transformed to a turbine powered mill. It is awaiting restoration.

Photos Courtesy of Authors

Saw and gristmill, East Vassalboro, Maine. The sawmill was built about 1797, the gristmill in 1810. They were joined to form a large commercial sawmill. The wheels were replaced by a pair of turbines. The gristmill is still operable, but the mill is primarily engaged in the sawing operation. It is the only large commercial waterpowered sawmill still in operation in the Northeast. The mill is now run by the Masse family. Louis Masse, a mill buff, insists that a waterpowered mill is economically viable and truly competitive with those powered by electricity or diesel engines.

Photo Courtesy of Louis Masse

Contemporary view.
Photo Courtesy of Authors

Sawmill, South Lee, New Hampshire. In ruins, this mill shared the dam with Harvey's mills. It was powered by a turbine. Some of the equipment remains.
Photo Courtesy of Authors

The idea of using waterpower to drive a saw is believed to have come from Scandinavia. Strangely enough, the English were among the last to adapt waterpower to sawing, perhaps because of riots that broke out when sawyers' jobs were threatened.

Some of the earliest references to sawmills in colonial America mention these mills:

YORK, MAINE	1623
PORTSMOUTH, NEW HAMPSHIRE	1631
SCITUATE, MASSACHUSETTS	1640
SILVERMINE, CONNECTICUT	1688

The first waterpowered sawmills were of the up and down variety. The vertical blade was about six feet long and six inches wide with a series of jagged teeth spaced about two inches apart. The blade was attached to a hardwood frame that moved up and down between notched, greased side blocks called fender posts, which steadied its motion. The saw frame was attached to a crank by a long rod called the pitman rod. The crank was geared to the waterpower or attached directly to the waterwheel shaft, depending on the type of waterwheel used. Although overshot wheels were used, the most common type of wheel in the up and down sawmill, before the turbine, was the flutter wheel. Its size was determined by the amount of water available. The ideal speed of the saw was about one hundred twenty strokes per minute. This, of course, varied when an extra thick piece of hardwood was being cut.

The sawyers were, like the millers, experts in their field. They knew what timber was best suited for a given purpose. They knew types of woods, how hard they were, when they should be harvested, how they should be cured, their flexibility, their strength, general appearance, and uses. The earliest mills were simple sawmills producing rough-cut boards marked by a series of uniform vertical scratches.

In 1810 Sister Tabitha Babbitt of the Harvard Shaker community, while watching her spinning wheel, conceived of a circular saw blade that if powered by water could cut planks at a much greater speed than the vertical blade.* This revolutionized the sawmill and to a certain extent led to more sophisticated machinery and specialized enterprises such as the planing mill, which produced smooth boards, the turning mill, which turned wood for columns, furniture legs, and so on, and specialty mills, which could cut anything to order from broom handles to bobbins.

The skills of the early blacksmith were also needed in millwrighting. He had to fashion all the iron parts of the mill. The crank was usually beyond the capabilities of the early smithies and had to be obtained from the furnaces.

---

* John G. Shea, *The American Shakers and Their Furniture*. New York: Van Nostrand Reinhold Co., 1971.

This page and following page: Three views of the up and down sawmill, Shelburne, Vermont. This mill came from Mill Brook Farm in South Royalton, Vermont. It was built about 1786 by Jeremiah Trescott of Hanover, New Hampshire.

Photos Courtesy Shelburne Museum, Shelburne, Vermont

EARLY AMERICAN MILLS

Chaney up and down sawmill, Old Sturbridge Village, Massachusetts. The machinery is from
Gilead, Connecticut.   *Photo Courtesy of Authors*

Left: Shown are the old fender posts, blade, hardwood frame, the arm that transmits motion from the saw frame to the feed pole, and the log held in place by hinged dogs and resting on the carriage. Chaney up and down sawmill.

Photo Courtesy of Authors

Above: Up and down sawmill, Greene, Rhode Island. This mill was moved from Hopkinton, Massachusetts, to its present location.

Photo Courtesy of Authors

Left: A portion of an up and down sawmill at Weston, Vermont, located in the Vermont Guild Museum. Shown is the blade, saw frame, hinged dogs with adjustable screws, feed pole, and the carriage track, which is upside down.

Photo Courtesy of Authors

Left: Taylor up and down sawmill, East Derry, New Hampshire, c. 1805. Original wood wheel has been replaced by iron one.
Photo Courtesy of Authors

Below: Sawmill, East Vassalboro, Maine. See p. 56.
Photo Courtesy of Louis Masse

The machinery in the early sawmills was placed in the center of a long low building, which had to be twice the size of the longest log. The log to be cut was placed on a sliding carriage, consisting of two rails with a heavy crossbeam at either end. The front beam was movable and could be adjusted to the length of the log. The log sat on these crossbeams and was held in place by a series of hinged dogs or iron clamps that could be adjusted by screws. The adjusting screws moved the log sideways to set the thickness of the board. The carriage rolled on wheels. The underside of the carriage had a series of teeth along its length. The teeth meshed with the gears of a wheel turned by a shaft from the waterwheel. At the other side of the mill was a large wheel, an iron hoop with jagged teeth called the rack wheel. The feed pole fed the log to the saw by the action of the rack wheel, which at one end was attached to the saw frame. When the saw cut, it moved the feed pole, which turned the rack wheel, inching the carriage ahead and delivering the log to the blade. The feed pole could be adjusted to determine the rate of advance of the log. It was also used as a stopping device to shut down the mill. Once the saw was set in motion, the cutting was totally automated. It gave the miller lots of free time.

To return the log for the next cut, a tub waterwheel was geared to the carriage. As the log returned, all the sawyer did was adjust the screws and all was ready for the next cut.

When the circular saw arrived it not only speeded production but eliminated items like the crank. It was geared directly to the wheel with the most force, usually an overshot wheel or turbine. Another benefit of the circular saw was that it decreased the wobble of the vertical blade. The wobble created a thick cut, often wasting precious inches of a log. The signature of the circular blade is a serious of curves on the board. The blade developed rapidly from solid iron to a combination of iron with steel cutting teeth inserted in the disk. There was great danger in this system—the teeth often flew out, maiming the sawyer. Finally, the all-steel blade was developed. It was the same type we use today.

The building housing these mills was constructed in a simple functional style like the gristmill. Often additions to existing gristmills created the sawmill. The sawmill by itself was open on either end and often on a third side as well. It was usually a single-gabled building. The enclosed side was where the waterwheel or turbine was placed. The other two or three sides were used to roll lumber into and out of the mill. The long open facade faced the road where a simple inclined plane or ramp was used to roll the logs into the mill. The building itself was frame and held together with mortise joints. The frame was covered with vertical boards. The overhang on the roof protected the sides from rain and snow. Occasionally clapboard was used. There was no heating system for fear of fire and lack of any enclosed space to heat. Basically sawmills were rough structures thrown together only to protect the machinery.

Before continuing our study of early waterpowered mills, a discussion of windmills will be helpful since they were used almost exclusively as grist and sawmills in America.

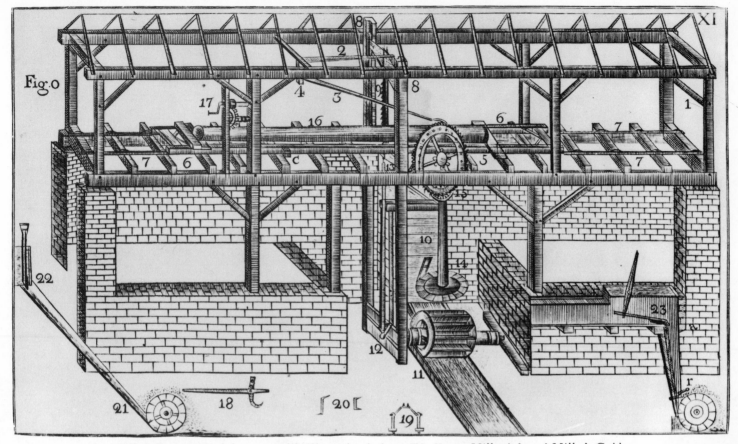

Oliver Evans up and down sawmill. Illustration is from *The Young Millwright and Miller's Guide*.
(1) Frame here is 52 feet long, 12 feet wide; (2) arm transmits motion from saw frame to feed
pole and on to carriage; (3) feed pole; (4) upper end of feed pole attached to arm that receives
motion of saw frame; (5) rack wheel; (6) carriage; (7) carriage track; (8) fender posts;
(9) blade and hardwood frame; (10) water; (11) flutter wheel; (12) crank attached to flutter
wheel; (13) pitman rod attached to crank; (14) tub wheel; (15) gearing of tub wheel to carriage
(cog wheel); (16) log to be sawed; (17) crank and windlass to bring logs into the mill; (18) cant
hook used to move logs; (19), (20) dogs; (21), (22) sluice gate, sluiceway, and flutter wheel.
Photo Courtesy Hagley Museum and Eleutherian Mills Historical Library, Greenville, Delaware

Carman's sawmill, Valley Stream, Long Island, New York. Destroyed.

Photo Courtesy Nassau County Historical Museum

Sawmill, New Milford, Connecticut, c. 1800. Destroyed.

Photo Courtesy of New Milford Historical Society

This lovely barn-red mill is situated in the town of New Preston, Connecticut, on the East Aspetuck River. It was built on the site of an old iron furnace that operated as far back as the 1700s. In the Civil War period Oscar Beeman chose this spot to build a sawmill and carpentry shop. It is now the home of Robert Woodruff and his family. According to Mr. Woodruff, Oscar Beeman was a local master builder, some of whose barns can still be found in the surrounding area. They are recognized by their characteristic cupolas. The same techniques were used to build the barns here and the mill. First the building's frame was erected. Then the sides, complete with windows, were constructed on the ground and raised into place by horses and men. This was the focal activity of the barn-raising celebrations of the past. Mr. Woodruff testified to the accuracy of Mr. Beeman's calculations by pointing out that to this day, winter or summer, wet or dry, his windows never stick. Mr. Woodruff bought the mill in 1941 from Oscar Beeman's son Henry, who made violins and cellos. Until a few years ago, Mr. Woodruff used the East Aspetuck's water to run a tool and machine shop. Today the turbine can still function. But this mill is the last of twenty-one mills and factories that once lived on the banks of the river, and it too has been threatened by the expansion of Route 25. This is one of the most beautiful mills that remains in all the Northeast. *Photo Courtesy of Authors*

Waterpowered sawmill, Irasburg, Vermont.

Photo Courtesy of Authors

Francis J. Morris sawmill, Wilton, New Hampshire. A turbine powered mill, with much of its equipment remaining, awaiting restoration.

Above: Cold Spring Harbor sawmill, Cold Spring Harbor, Long Island, New York, c. 1880. Destroyed.
Photo courtesy Nassau County Historical Museum

WINDMILLS

Perhaps the most beautiful of all structures harnessing natural power is the windmill. In many countries it was used to grind grain, pump seawater into evaporation vats to make salt, saw wood and perform other tasks. Wind power has certain advantages over waterpower. Icing, dry spells, tide tables, and the constant replacement of waterwheels because of rot all vanished. These many concerns were replaced by the fear of being caught with sails up in gale-force winds or of not having enough wind to turn the sails. Locations were carefully selected for strong and steady wind. Expanses of cleared flatland, a high hill, or open areas by the sea were particularly favored. In colonial days, the coasts of Rhode Island, Cape Cod, and Long Island Sound were especially suited to windmills, and that is where they survive today. A well-constructed windmill could operate with as little wind as would not blow out a candle.

The origin of the windmill is not at all clear. Recent evidence attributes its discovery to Persia or China. Whether the idea traveled to Europe via the East or was spontaneously invented in various places is subject to debate and speculation. In any case, by the twelfth century windmills had begun to appear in England and northern Europe. The idea was brought to America and developed rapidly by both English and Dutch settlers. By the mid-seventeenth century windmills are known to have been in operation in Massachusetts and New York. Early drawings of New Amsterdam show large numbers of windmills built by the Dutch who first colonized Manhattan. In fact, part of the seal of New York consists of the vanes of a windmill. Laws were even passed that acknowledged their presence. In 1680 no person could cross from New York to Brooklyn in a rowboat when the sails of the windmills had been taken in. This was a seventeenth century small-craft warning that winds were too high.

It is thought that early windmills were built by seamen and shipwrights because many of the fundamentals of sailing apply to the functions of windmills. The windmiller would need to know not only the particulars of sawyering or grist grinding, but he would have to have a knowledge of the construction, repair, and the use of sails, which necessitated an understanding of wind dynamics, carpentry, mechanics, and engineering, as well as an eye for the weather. It is true that help and advice came from local carpenters, but it must not have been rare for one man to be knowledgeable in all aspects of building and operating windmills.

The basic mechanics and driving mechanisms of the windmill are the same as those of the water mill, except that the waterwheel is replaced by huge arms with sails. The shaft that holds the waterwheel and the face wheel is comparable to the wind shaft connecting the rotating arms to the rest of the machinery.

The Pantigo mill, East Hampton, Long Island, New York. Built, or possibly rebuilt, in 1771 for Abram Gardiner.   *Photo Courtesy of Authors*

▶

Gardiner mill, East Hampton, Long Island, New York. This gristmill (windmill) was built in 1771.

Photo Courtesy of Authors

There were two basic types of windmills used in America. The earliest type was the post-mill. It was quite rare, and to our knowledge none have survived in the Northeast. The entire mill and its works were housed in a large square box placed on top of a post. The box revolved on a tallowed wooden collar on the post so that the sails could face into the wind. The mill was revolved when a man wheeled the tailpiece, a long pole running from the box to a wheel on the ground, into place.

The central post was supported by massive timbers called quarter boards and heavy crosstrees. The mill had to be elevated to allow clearance for the sails, and a man could only enter by a ladder. Small holes were punched in the boxlike structure so that the miller could determine the direction of the wind. In some instances, a sack hoist was attached to the wind shaft.

The post-mill had many drawbacks, particularly the lack of storage space. It was replaced by the smock mill, so called because of its resemblance to a smock or loose garment. The important innovation was a cap that could be turned by a wind mechanism, winch, or by a lever and wheel like the tailpiece of the post-mill, rather than the whole mill. The smock mill could be very large with considerable interior space. It most resembled a tall wooden tower on an octagonal plan and was commonly covered with shingles. The mill itself had eight enormous vertical posts, one in each corner rising to the height of the tower and all resting on wooden sills. The sides had horizontal framing reinforced with diagonal braces to provide the strength needed to withstand the force of the

Post Mill

1. Wagon wheel that rotates the mill attached to the tailpiece
2. Ladder
3. Main post
4. Quarter boards
5. Porick pier
6. Retaining sleeve
7. Crosstree
8. Entrance
9. Millhouse
10. Sail stock
11. Wagon-wheel track

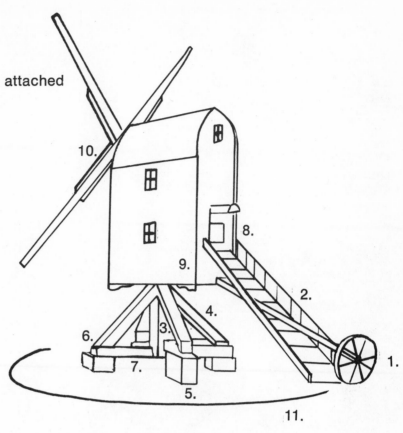

Portsmouth gristmill, Portsmouth, Rhode Island. A smock windmill using a winch to turn its cap. Totally reconstructed on its present site based on a mill c. 1790.

Photo Courtesy of Authors

►

Chatham gristmill, Chatham, Massachusetts, 1797. A smock windmill using a lever and wheel (tailpiece and wagon wheel) to move the cap into the wind. *Photo Courtesy of Authors*

Wind-powered gristmill, Water
Mill, Long Island, New York.
Photo Courtesy of Authors

revolving sails, even in gale-force winds, and to provide a support for the
revolving cap, the wind shaft, and vanes. The cap when dome-shaped was
constructed of a series of beams mortised to the top of the cap and radiating to
the horizontal framing at the base. The dome cap was pierced at either end by
the wind shaft and winch. Caps took on other shapes such as a sort of rounded
gable and often were slightly inclined from front to rear. When used to grind
grain the smock mill could operate a number of stones simultaneously. Within
both kinds of windmills there were certain common features. The large break
wheel's function was twofold. It was comparable to the face wheel of the waterwheel in that it was attached to the main shaft turned by the sails. It was geared
to a wallower that in the gristmill turned the spindle. Around the circumference
of the enormous break wheel was a wooden band or brake that was tightened by
a pulley or lever to stop the wheel by friction. At first all parts were made of
wood, but as iron technology advanced wood gave way to metal.

A further refinement of the system of adjusting the cap into the wind
came with the device of the fantail or flier. It was a smaller windwheel attached
on the cap opposite the large sail arms. As the wind shifted the flier turned the
cap, keeping it properly facing the wind.

EARLY AMERICAN MILLS

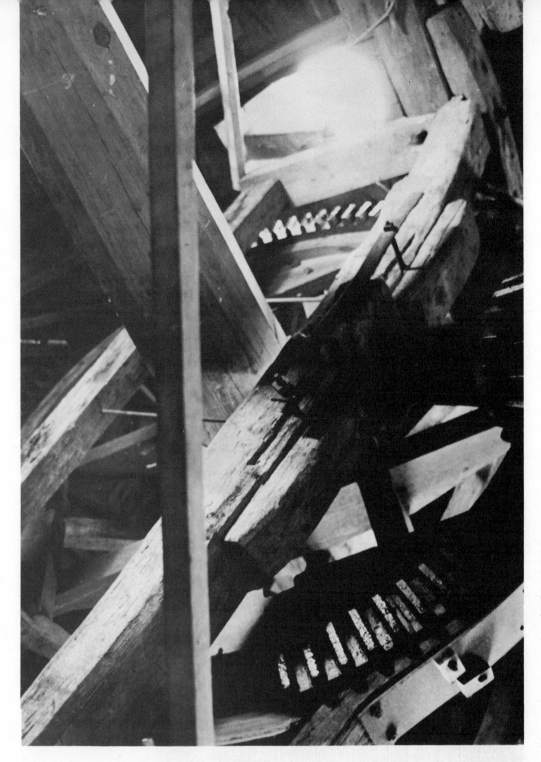

Interiors of Jamestown grist (wind) mill, Jamestown, Rhode Island, 1787. Note the great brake wheel, brake shoe, and wind shaft.

Photo Courtesy of Authors

Note the great brake wheel (face wheel) geared to the wallower (iron gear has replaced a wooden lantern gear), which turns the spindle.

Photo Courtesy of Authors

Note the hole in the runner stone; the grappling hook was inserted there.

Photo Courtesy of Authors

Note grappling hooks for raising the runner stone and a corn sheller.

Photo Courtesy of Authors

Eastham windmill, Eastham, Massachusetts, 1793, Cape Cod's oldest windmill. Note its conical cap and large brake handle protruding from it. The rope attached to the brake handle allowed control of the sails from outside the mill.

Photo Courtesy of Authors

a. Flyer
b. Brake wheel
c. Gear that revolves the cap
d. Stones
e. Wind shaft

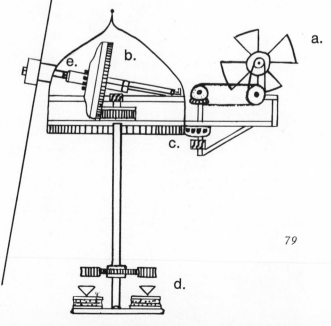

79

Bridgehampton mill (Beebe gristmill), Bridgehampton, Long Island, New York, 1820. Originally built at Sag Harbor in 1820, this is the only windmill left in the Northeast that has a flywheel. Note the beautiful whale weather vane. When a whale ship entered the harbor, a flag was raised on the mill. So came the adage "flag on the mill, ship in the bay." Another unusual feature is that the millstones revolve ten times for one complete turn of a sail arm instead of the usual six.

Photo Courtesy of Authors

SAILS

Sails were of heavy cotton duck canvas. As in the Dutch tradition, they were stretched over wooden vanes, usually four in number, which were constructed of strong, light wood. They consisted of lengthwise members called whips or uplongs that were met at right angles by sail bars. This gridlike structure was attached to a stock, a tapering shaft mortised or wedged at its widest end to the wind shaft.

The plane in which the sails rotated was inclined enabling them to catch more wind. When the mill was not in use the sails were furled or removed entirely. This was a tedious job as the sails were enormous, often as much as sixty feet long. When the wind started blowing, much force was exerted, some of which was absorbed by the structure.

Jamestown gristmill, Jamestown, Rhode Island, 1787. Note the whips and sail bars attached to the stocks, which are attached to the wind shaft.

Photo Courtesy of Authors

Hook mill, East Hampton, Long Island, New York. Built by Nathaniel Doming in 1796. Note the gabled type cap and the attached sails.

Photo Courtesy Nassau County Historical Museum

East Marion mill, East Marion, Long Island, New York, c. 1800. This old photograph shows the mill under sail.
Photo Courtesy Nassau County Historical Museum

Hicks mill, Westbury, Long Island, New York. Note unusual sail arrangement.
Photo Courtesy Nassau County Historical Museum

Old Slater mill, Pawtucket, Rhode Island. Now a textile museum full of wonderful machinery. The building has undergone much alteration since the time of Almy and Brown.   *Photo Courtesy of Authors*

Bell cupola of the Cheshire mill, Harrisville, New Hampshire.
Photo Courtesy of Authors

Boardinghouse and colony residence, Harrisville, New Hampshire.
Photo Courtesy of Authors

This old type of vane and sail was later superseded in England in 1807 by a shutter type, which, like a venetian blind, could be opened and closed. When closed it acted like a canvased vane, when open, as a braking mechanism by letting the wind blow through unresisted. All the old windmills standing that we encountered are of the earlier variety. The shutter type is still being used today, especially in the West, to pump water. During high winds great care had to be exercised not to brake too quickly as friction could create fire. Once the mill caught fire it would be impossible to salvage it. At the other extreme, if proper braking did not take place, the vanes would act as propellers and tear the mill to pieces. It is clear that windmills were always tricky and could be dangerous.

When the windmill was used as a sawmill, a crank wheel mounted on a crankshaft meshed with the wallower, which was geared to the wind shaft. The crankshaft was hooked directly to the saw frames. The remaining mechanism was exactly the same as in the waterpowered mill.

The windmill was also used to pump seawater, the method by which Holland was reclaimed from the sea. Although such mills probably existed in the early days in America, none of them remain. In Europe windmills were also used to pump wells, to drive textile machinery, to press oil, and to perform other tasks. Numerous improvements made them efficient power sources. In early America only small windmills were used and in a fairly limited way. When knowledge of the improvements arrived alternative power sources had already been more highly developed.

IRONWORKS

The need for iron was always great. In the early days of the new nation, all iron was imported from the mother country. Being dependent on Europe was costly and burdensome. Prices rose as ore and timber deposits were depleted. Shipping charges had to be paid and deliveries were sporadic. People needed hammers, wheel hoops, saw blades, knives, pots, and hundreds of other tools and utensils. Numerous deposits of ore were discovered in the colonies and, finally, some furnaces were built. The first was believed to be at Falling Creek, Virginia. Its operation abruptly ceased when the Indians massacred all the workers. Other attempts were made, such as the one in 1644 by John Winthrop, future entrepreneur and governor of Connecticut. This enterprise at Braintree, Massachusetts, lasted about three years and failed because of insufficient waterpower and ore. The group of investors organized by Winthrop tried again. This time they hired Richard Leader who completed some of the building at Braintree but quickly persuaded the company to back an enterprise on the Saugus River.

SAUGUS IRONWORKS

The site he chose was perfect, having ample bog and rock ore nearby. Water was available for power and navigation. A natural elevation for the charging

View of furnace bridge, furnace forge, rolling and slitting mills, Saugus ironworks, Saugus, Massachusetts.
Photo Courtesy of Authors

Saugus ironworks. Overall view of forge and rolling and slitting mill.
Photo Courtesy of Authors

bridge, stocks of ample timber and the availability of labor all were there. The works constructed consisted of a furnace, finery and chaffery hearths, a rolling and slitting mill, and charcoal mounds. Housing was built and workers from England imported. Local help was used for numerous tasks not requiring expertise, such as tree felling, stocking, and ore digging. And finally a town called Hammersmith developed around the works. Labor was in such scarce supply that three thousand Scots taken prisoner by Cromwell at the battle of Dunbar were sold into indentured service to the works. The ironworkers did not mix well with Puritan society; many were less than religious—a rude, brawling, drinking group. Records tell of numerous men being put in jail. Accidents were frequent and many a man maimed; the air was foul and full of soot. But the works were built and were as good as any in the mother country.

IRONMAKING

The ironmaking, casting, and milling processes started in the bogs and open-pit mines and forests. Enormous quantities of wood were needed and many a forest was felled. The wood was piled into kilns, enormous mounds of stone covered with sod. Through a slow-burning process, taking up to ten days from start to finish, the wood was converted into charcoal.

Ore was gathered from the bogs and pits and transported to the furnace. The final ingredient was flux, a material needed to remove impurities from the bog ore; limestone or *gabbio* was often used.

The typical furnace, built of stone and mortared with clay, varied in height

Wassaic charcoal kilns, 1863, south of Amenia, New York. Made charcoal for local blast furnaces.

Photo Courtesy of Authors

Right: Large bellows for furnace at Saugus.
Photo Courtesy of Authors

Below: Interior charcoal kiln.
Photo Courtesy of Authors

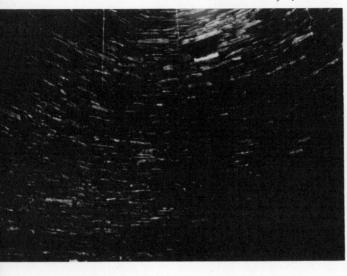

Right: Casting floor and entrance to crucible,
Saugus ironworks.
Photo Courtesy of Authors

from twenty to forty feet. At the National Parks Service restoration at Saugus the large furnace measures twenty-six feet square at the base and is twenty-one feet high. It is shaped somewhat like a truncated pyramid on the outside. The interior of the furnace is bottle shaped and sometimes lined with firebrick or refractory sandstone. At the top is a hole called the charge hole into which the charge of ore, charcoal, and flux is shoveled in layers. Directly beneath the hole at the bottom of the furnace is the crucible, which is lined with heat-resistant material such as refractory sandstone. Into the crucible flows the molten metal as it is formed from the charge above. The impurities, called slag, rise to the top and are skimmed off. Outside the furnace is a trench with a waterwheel that pumps

Iron furnace, East Dorset, Vermont.
Photo Courtesy of Authors
▶

Richmond furnace, near Richmond, Massachusetts.
Photo Courtesy of Authors

two huge leather bellows, sending a steady stream of air to the furnace through a pipe called the tuyere. Special care has to be taken to drain water from the wheel away from the furnace because if even a small amount of water reaches the molten metal an explosion would occur. Water contacting the extremely high temperature of the iron (around 2,200°F) would turn to steam, releasing energy that would splatter the hot metal.

The furnace was tapped twice a day to obtain the iron and remove the slag that had floated to the top of the liquid metal. The iron was run off into furrows where it cooled into bars of pig iron or was cast directly into molds for various items.

The furnace ran constantly and only shut down when the wheels froze, for major repairs, or for cleaning. The workers' lives revolved around this fiery monster that had to be constantly fed and tapped.

Richmond furnace counting-house. Notice the octagonal glass cupola; it provided continuous, even light for the. agents' book-keeping tasks.
Photo Courtesy of Authors

Kent furnace, Kent, Connecticut.
Photo Courtesy of Authors

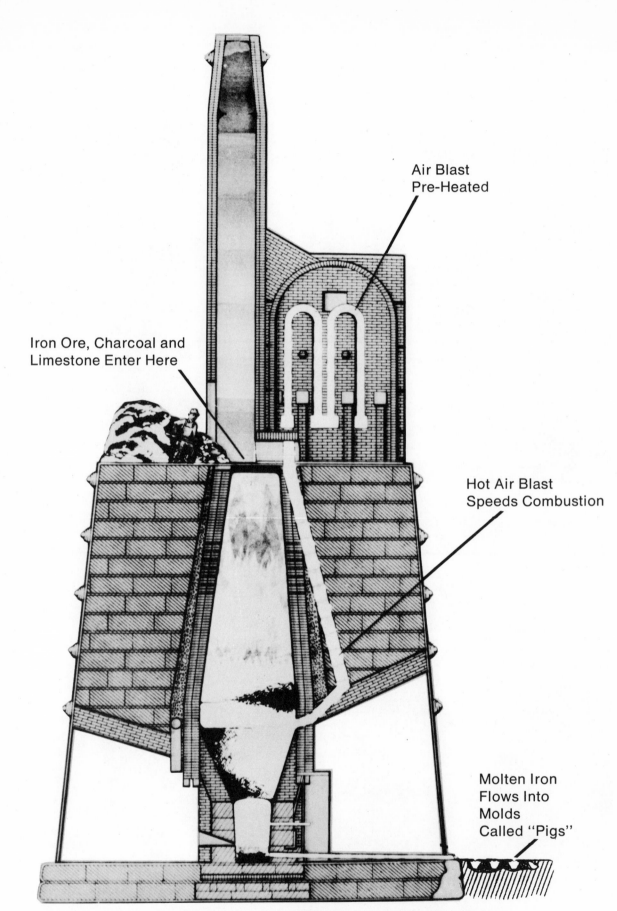

Air Blast
Pre-Heated

Iron Ore, Charcoal and
Limestone Enter Here

Hot Air Blast
Speeds Combustion

Molten Iron
Flows Into
Molds
Called "Pigs"

Diagram of the Kent furnace. This photograph was taken of a three-dimensional diagram on display
at the Sloane-Stanley Museum, Kent, Connecticut.   *Photo Courtesy Sloane-Stanley Museum*

Right: Copake iron furnace, Copake Falls, New York, 1846, located in Taconic State Park. The original furnace was replaced in 1872 by the one shown here. At that time it was a huge works consisting of twenty residences for workers and their families and nine company buildings. The company reached its zenith in 1880 and operated intermittently until World War I. A few of the buildings remain. From notes provided by the New York State Historic Trust.

Photo Courtesy of Authors

Below: Chatham iron furnace, Chatham, New York, 1893.
Photo Courtesy of Authors

Left: Dover furnace, Sharparoon, New York, 1881. Note the beautiful gothic arch giving access to the crucible and hearth.

Photo Courtesy of Authors

Below: Interior of the Dover furnace.

Photo Courtesy of Authors

MacIntyre ironworks, at the deserted village of Adirondac, New York. The following information is from notes given to us by the New York State Historic Trust.

An "iron dam," a fifty-foot vein of rich magnetic ore, was discovered here by Archibald MacIntyre, Duncan McMartin, and David Henderson. They slowly developed an industrial community in the Adirondack wilderness called Adirondac, or MacIntyre, and established the first iron forge in 1832, a cupola furnace about 1837, and the first blast furnace in 1844.

The enterprise grew and prospered from 1845 to 1853. Joseph Dixon, famous for his work with crucibles of graphite, was hired to make steel from pig iron produced in the MacIntyre furnaces. The first American-made steel was turned out in Jersey City in 1851.

A new furnace was ordered in 1852. Measuring 36 inches square and 48 inches high, it had a capacity of 14 tons of pig iron a day. It is probably the best-preserved iron furnace stack in New York State and still has the hot blast ovens mounted on top of the stone stack and also portions of the cast-iron conductor pipes.

The great furnace operated only two years before the syndicate failed. Transportation difficulties and the death of the owners brought about the change in fortune.

The site was converted in the 1870s to a private hunting and fishing club called Old Tahawus. The earliest wooden structure, the McNaughton house, to which was added a small lean-to known as MacIntyre Bank, was the site Vice-President Theodore Roosevelt was visiting at the time of the assassination of President McKinley. From that spot he started his journey to Buffalo and the Presidency. *Photo Courtesy of Authors*

Saugus ironworks, Saugus, Massachusetts. Restoration opened in 1954. A hammer rests on an iron bar, which rests on the anvil. The hammer is attached to an oak beam called a "helve." Cams attached to a waterwheel shaft are visible directly behind the great hammer. The helve is inserted in a "hurst," or band, which had two projections called pivots that rested and turned in iron cradles set into heavy timbers. Above the helve is a large timber called the stop, which hit the helve as it was released by the cam, providing the downward hammer blow with extra force.

Photo Courtesy of Authors

FORGES

Not all furnaces were coupled with forges. Most simply sold their pig iron to blacksmiths or made castings. They were equipped with casting floors that contained molds of standard items such as stoves and kettles and later on machine parts. Many of these small operations functioned well into the late nineteenth century. The iron industry eventually gravitated toward Pennsylvania when coal came into use. To this day, our principal iron and steel mills are located there.

Some furnaces like the Saugus reconstruction also had forges for forming wrought iron in various shapes. Pig iron had to pass through various stages before it became a wrought-iron form. First it was reheated and melted and combined with oxygen to remove impure carbon. This took place on the finery hearth. The chaffery hearth was used to further heat and refine the iron for the final pounding into merchant bars. At Saugus the hammer used at this stage has a massive iron head weighing five hundred pounds. It is attached to a stout oak beam called the helve, and is powered by a fourteen-foot pitch-back wheel that uses a series of cams to raise the hammer.

The iron-making procedure was lengthy and dangerous. Sparks flew and hammers swung, often burning and maiming. Men wielded heavy tools such as iron tongs six feet in length to carry heavy bars of iron, often weighing over one hundred and fifty pounds. The buildings were poorly ventilated, and during the summer became infernally hot. Men often collapsed, muscles were torn, and lungs were ruined from smoke and gases. Life was not easy for the men who worked the forges.

ROLLING AND SLITTING MILLS

The important furnaces had rolling and slitting mills as well as forges. Here were formed items that could be cut or slit from iron, which had been rolled into flat sheets. Such items were nails, wheel hoops, barrel bands, and so on.

The only example of this mill that we found is at the Saugus reconstructed iron works. There, two seventeen-foot overshot wheels drive a pair of rollers used to flatten the heated iron bars and a set of disk cutters that slit the flattened bars into strips.

An ingenious gearing system is installed that rotates one roller and one disk in the opposite direction from its mate but at the same speed. On the shaft of one wheel cams operate heavy shears, which nip the iron merchant bars that are heated in a nearby hearth.

Iron furnaces were established on rivers all over the Northeast from the 1600s on. Cast iron came into wide use in the first quarter of the nineteenth century, and millowners began to replace the more vulnerable wooden wheels and gears with iron ones, and metal turbines began to replace the more picturesque wheel. Iron was also widely used in machine building, particularly in the booming textile industry.

Saugus ironworks. The foreground shows two overshot wheels used for the rolling and slitting mill. The wheel in the background ran the bellows in the forge.

Photo Courtesy of Authors

Two overshot wheels of rolling and slitting mill at the Saugus ironworks.
Photo Courtesy of Authors

Saugus ironworks. Bellows operated by waterwheel. Note cam attached to waterwheel shaft.
Photo Courtesy of Authors

SNUFF MILLS

Snuff, like tobacco, is said to have originated with the American Indians. By the late seventeenth and early eighteenth century snuff was all the rage in Europe. Fashion in Europe spread to America, and soon it seemed profitable to establish a snuff mill. This was done for the first time in North Kingston, Rhode Island, on Petaquamscott Pond by two gentlemen, Dr. Thomas Moffatt and Gilbert Stuart, father of the great early American painter of the same name. The artist, having been brought up in a snuff mill, became a snuff addict. When we visited the place and watched the grinding for a few minutes, the raised dust powder was easily discernible and had us sneezing away. Finding out about Gilbert Stuart's addiction was no surprise. Mr. Stuart's establishment was yet another example of an economic independence that did not find favor with the British. His operation was considered illegal, and, among other miseries, the Scottish sheep's bladder used to hold the snuff was forbidden importation.

Snuff is made by grinding tobacco leaves and stalks in a mortar and pestle. The leaves and stalks are aged for several years and then fermented. This removes excess acid and oils and a large portion of the nicotine. The mixture is dried, ground to powder, and mixed with spices such as cloves, lavender, and cassia, which causes the brown powder to smell delicious. It was placed in

Snuff mill (Gilbert Stuart Homestead), North Kingston, Rhode Island, c. 1750.
Photo Courtesy of Authors

The face wheel drives a small gear, which turns the lantern gear to which is attached the pestle.

Photo Courtesy of Authors

fancy snuffboxes or on handkerchiefs, and was thought to be a panacea, curing everything from heartburn to athlete's foot. It was expensive and had snob appeal.

Gilbert Stuart's snuff mill is a simple affair consisting of a waterwheel with a shaft running into the first floor of the Stuart's residence, a beautiful three-storied gambrel-roofed house. The mill was located on the ground floor as was the main cooking hearth. The snuff mill is essentially a waterpowered mortar and pestle. The waterwheel is outside. The face wheel is indoors connected to the main shaft, which was geared to a lantern gear or wallower. The shaft running through and turned by the wallower extended down and to the side, terminating in the pestle. As the lantern gear revolved, the pestle's end rotated within the mortar that was firmly fixed. Snuff making was automated, because a great amount of grinding and pulverizing was required to turn tobacco into snuff.

On the same property once stood a sawmill, fulling mill, and gristmill (see page 43). Parts of the gristmill still remain.

Franklin cider mill, Franklin, Connecticut, c. 1890. Apples
fall through hopper onto pressing table. Table slides under the
press (in the background).   *Photo Courtesy of Authors*

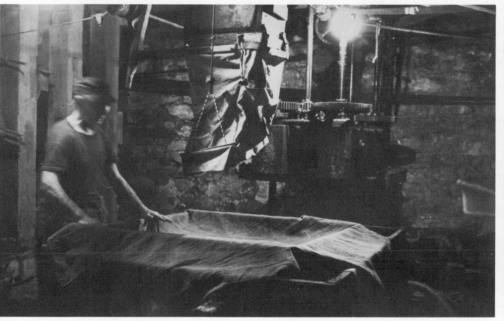

CIDER MILLS

Every fall, around the first of October, waterpowered cider mills all over
America used to start pressing apples. In our quest for such mills we found only
one that still functioned by waterpower alone. The Franklin cider mill, Franklin,
Connecticut, established around 1890 and operated by Arthur Conrad Carlson,
is a simple functional mill powered by a turbine that delivers approximately
twenty horsepower. The process of making cider is fairly simple. Apples are
carted to the mill's upper floor, which faces the roadway. Mr. Carlson insists
that only McIntosh apples make superb cider.

At his mill the apples are dumped into a hopper and chute and released to
the floor below. They fall on a pressing table, which is swung under a press that
operates like a book press or giant screw. A tough burlap is used as a sieve. When
the sluiceway is opened the turbine is set in motion. A series of gears and pulleys
lowers the press with a force that Mr. Carlson puts at fifty tons. The machinery

Benkert's cider mill, Bethpage,
Long Island, New York, 1888.
Built by George Benkert.
*Photo Courtesy Nassau County
Historical Museum*

is controlled by levers right next to the press. The sweet cider flows into a trough and is pumped upstairs into kegs to be bottled and sold, or kept to make hard cider for those who find that a more enjoyable brew.

FULLING MILLS

When woolen cloth came off the loom it had a loose weave, was dirty, and generally unattractive. Fulling was the process that, when carefully controlled, cleaned, felted, and shrank the cloth. Cloth was placed in a vat of water with some detergent or caustic substance such as animal urine or fuller's earth. The cloth was pounded, wrung, and turned, and again pounded and wrung until the desired consistency was attained.

In Egypt, Rome, and old Europe, the cloth was usually tread upon like wine. The word to "full" comes from Old French *fuler*, meaning to tread or walk upon. (The surname Walker is derived from this occupation.)

Fulling was the first process in the manufacture of woolen cloth that was to benefit from waterpower.

In early fulling mills a shaft was connected to a waterwheel at one end and had a set of cams at the other that raised a large wooden hammer. These were released into troughs containing the cloth and solutions. As the hammers hit the cloth they turned it, constantly changing the area being struck. This was a long and tedious process that was finally replaced by a circular fulling machine that was perfected by 1830.

FOLLI PER FOLAR PANNI DI LANA ET ALTRO

The fulling machine shows a waterwheel using cams to drive fulling stocks. A man carries cloth to be fulled. Unpublished monograph plate taken from *Zonca-Novo Teatro di machine, e edificii*, Padua, 1607; included in a report by Sally G. Farris for the Hagley Museum, 1956–1960.

Photo Courtesy Hagley Museum, Wilmington, Delaware

Above: Roller fulling machine. On display at the Merrimack Valley Textile Museum.   *Photo Courtesy of Authors*

Right: The roller fulling machine replaced the stock fulling machine and was commonly used in textile mills. Taken from *The Fulling Machine* by Sally G. Farris, Hagley Museum Report, 1956–1960. Unpublished monograph plate taken from *Knights American Mechanical Dictionary*, New York, 1877.

   Photo Courtesy Hagley Museum, Wilmington, Delaware

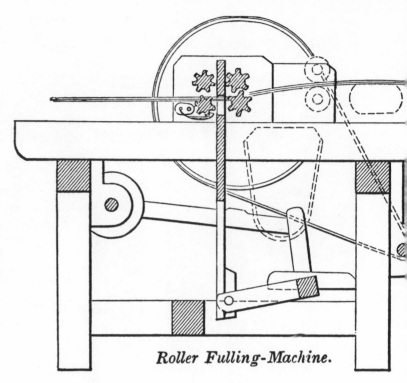

Roller Fulling-Machine.

The first waterpowered fulling mill in colonial America was erected in 1643 at Rowley, Massachusetts, by John Pearson. By 1810 there were about 1,682 fulling mills on record in America. Soon after this date the processing of woolen cloth was taken over by the factory system (see Part II). Yet there were still some one thousand fulling mills left in the 1880s.

The fulling mill shown here in the form of a painting is one where the process is almost entirely carried out by hand. Perhaps the stocks or rotary mills were below. In all our travels we never encountered a single fulling mill. It is true that all the woolen mills had fulling machines as part of their equipment, but of the hundreds of small, simple fulling mills, to our knowledge, not one has survived. The common practice, as time went on, was to install a fulling machine in a gristmill, benefiting from an existing power source.

CARDING MILLS

Carding is the process of straightening and untangling the fibers of a material, wool or cotton for example, before yarn can be spun. Long before the use of cotton became common (about the turn of the eighteenth century in America)

Fulling mill painted by James Walter Folger, 1911.
Photo Courtesy Society for the Preservation of New England Antiquities, Boston

wool carding was performed by hand. A prickly plant called teasle in English and *cardère* in French (from which comes the word "card") was used for this purpose. The plants were replaced by man-made brushes or cards. These were made of fine wire teeth set into leather or wood.

A skilled person could card only about one and a half pounds of wool per day with hand cards. Mechanized carding saved many hours of tedious labor. The carding machine marks a transition from home or domestic manufacture of both cotton and wool cloth to factory methods.

Several great English innovators of textile machinery experimented with the carding machine. Sir Richard Arkwright in 1775 produced the first fully mechanized carding machine. Due to England's stern restrictive policies, no machines or plans for textile machines were allowed to be exported. On several occasions, however, enterprising individuals relied on memory and Yankee ingenuity to re-create England's machines in her former colony. Plans for carding machines were smuggled into the states in 1794 in the memories of two English brothers, John and Arthur Schofield.

The carding machine consisted of a series of rollers of different sizes. These rollers were covered with leather stuck full of fine wire teeth. It was none other than Oliver Evans who invented a method for producing fifteen hundred card

Carding mill interior built in South Waterford, Maine, c. 1835. Moved to Old Sturbridge Village, Massachusetts, in 1963. The man in the photograph is holding a carded "lap" of cotton; to his left and right are carding machines.

Photo Courtesy of Authors

teeth per minute. Carding machines, like fulling machines, were often set up in existing water mills, especially gristmills. Occasionally they were housed in their own buildings and were geared to their own waterwheel. Housewives could bring their loose wool, send it through the machine, and go home with yards of long, soft-carded "lap" that was ready to be spun into yarn. Although carding mills, or other mills housing carding machines, were plentiful in 1810, we found only one, that has been transported to and rebuilt at Old Sturbridge Village. It is the Hopgood carding mill from South Waterford, Maine. It is run by a tub wheel geared to a drum wheel from which a belt rises to the upper floor and connects to the machine. The building is single-storied and clapboard-covered, with the wheel, gears, and driving machinery below.

2

TEXTILE MILLS

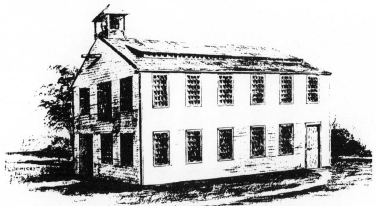

The Old Slater Mill, Pawtucket Rhode Island.

COTTON

THE FACTORY SYSTEM WAS AN OUTGROWTH OF THE ubiquitous domestic mills. A factory can be characterized as the building wherein manufacturing is carried on by machine methods, with the aim toward mass production. In the modern definition, a factory is thought of as the place where, under one roof, a product is processed from start to finish. This kind of organization was reached through several stages and depended upon a succession of mechanical inventions covering all processes for a given item. The Shakers, for example, invented and used certain machines powered by water in making their furniture. Yet these collectors' items are considered masterpieces of the hand-craftsman's art.

In both England and America the full-fledged factory evolved as a result of mechanization, especially in the cotton industry. As cotton textiles left the handcraft or home industry stage with the invention of machine processes, the industry experienced a tremendous boom. The first cotton mills led the way in all factory architecture and the communities associated with cotton manufacture were the first to feel the changes and problems of the industrial revolution. Indeed, cotton was the major contributor to it and for that reason, that industry and its architecture dominate our discussion of later industrial architecture.

In America two distinct patterns of early industrialization developed in the cotton industry: the Slater or southern New England style and the Waltham

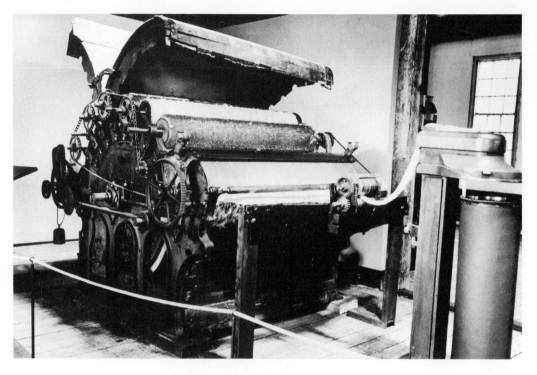

Carding machine from the 1820s showing the toothed cylinder and the carded lap issuing from the end. Carding was the first cotton process to be mechanized. The machine in the display is from the Old Slater Mill Textile Museum.

Photo Courtesy of Authors

plan. Descriptions of their development will be given separately, but comparisons will present themselves along the way.

Samuel Slater, a young Englishman, brought the first effective cotton technology to an America that knew little or nothing of industrialization. Born in 1768, he experienced the birth pangs of England's industrial revolution. Only a few months before, James Watt had been granted his steam-engine patent.

In 1767 James Hargreaves invented a machine to replace the age-old spinning wheel in the making of yarn or thread. The first spinning jenny, said to be named after Hargreaves' wife, was constructed mainly of wood and had eight spindles. The process of stretching and twisting the cotton into yarn occurred in eight places simultaneously, much to the astonishment of housewives and men of science alike. Further improvements expanded the jenny's capacity to eighty spindles. Hargreaves was also responsible for adapting the existing wool carding machine, with its toothed cylinders, to the carding of cotton. Thus, two intermediate steps—spinning and carding—in the complicated production of cotton cloth became mechanized.

It was Richard Arkwright, later knighted for his clever inventions, who brought all the steps of yarn making, with the exception of cotton cleaning or picking, to a level of mechanization through waterpower, which became known as the Arkwright system.

The soft lap of carded cotton was stretched and twisted into a loose, lumpy, and coarse preliminary yarn called a roving. The roving then passed to Sir Richard's own spinning invention based on a different principle from Hargreaves' and powered by water. This water frame passed the roving through a series of rollers that turned at graduated speeds, thereby providing the necessary stretch and twist to make the yarn of desired strength and fineness.

Samuel Slater spent six and a half of his young years apprenticed to a former partner of Arkwright's—Jedediah Strutt. There he undoubtedly had ample opportunity to develop his mechanical genius and to familiarize himself with the Arkwright system.

There were other inventors as well. Samuel Crompton had pushed spinning a step ahead by combining the techniques of Hargreaves' and Arkwright's machines. His mule produced an especially even and strong yarn.

Edmund Cartwright's power loom, although not altogether satisfactory, was beginning to make possible the practice of large-scale power weaving by 1787.

By the time Slater was ready to set out on his own, there were many textile mills in England's cities.

Left: A replica of Crompton's Mule of the 1780s. The wheel was turned by hand. Crompton later adapted spindle spinning to waterpower and this machine became obsolete. The machine in the display is from the Old Slater Mill Textile Museum.   *Photo Courtesy of Authors*

Above: Power loom in the Merrimack Valley Textile Museum.
Photo Courtesy of Authors

Left: Mule spinning machine from 1909 in the Old Slater Mill Textile Museum. This type of machine carried up to 180 spindles and reached a considerable length.
Photo Courtesy of Authors

Artist's rendering of the old Slater mill in Pawtucket where Samuel Slater introduced mechanized cotton spinning in America in the 1790s.
Photo Courtesy Old Slater Mill Textile Museum, Pawtucket, Rhode Island

Large textile cities were booming, smoky, crowded places where fortunes were being made by the few at the top, with pauper-house and orphanage labor toiling at the bottom. Steam power and the burning of dirty fuels were prevalent; cities such as Manchester were becoming a scandal.

Slater wished to go to America where it was known that some investors were most anxious to find trained mechanics who could make order out of their early attempts at machine building. England, who wished to keep her former colonies economically dependent as a supplier of raw material and a buyer of finished products, had stringent immigration restrictions on all persons acquainted with her industrial secrets. Neither were machines, plans, models, or drawings let out of the country. Slater reputedly managed to slip out disguised as a farm laborer, carrying plans, figures, and calculations in his head.

When he arrived in New York in 1789 at the age of twenty-one he found himself in a pioneering country entirely given over to agriculture and, in the seacoast towns, to commerce, shipping, and whaling. Manufactures were in the handcraft stage. The frontiersman wore his homespuns, either linens, woolens, or linsey-woolseys. Cotton was virtually nonexistent. Those who could afford it bought imported English yard goods of all kinds.

Everywhere Slater must have encountered the tough Yankee farmer whose distrust of manufacturing stemmed often from personal experience in the sweatshop of those grim factory cities of England. It was assumed by many of our puritanical forefathers that work in a factory was perdition itself. Nothing had yet developed here like the class structure of Britain. There was no urban proletariat. The frontier was the great leveler where a man was as good as his mind, his strength, and his terms with the Lord. Factory work would bring, it was assumed, a loss of rank and grace, especially to the "weaker sex."

Yet New England abounded in possible millsites: rivers, streams, and creeks were everywhere. The humidity of the air was considered an advantage because it helped prevent the delicate cotton threads from breaking during the spinning process. New England was the most thickly settled part of the country; her port cities promised the best transportation available, and it was there also that the largest amounts of capital were to be found.

Slater's quest for collaboration and backing in the cotton venture soon led him to the established Quaker merchant firm of Almy & Brown, based in Providence, Rhode Island. Moses Brown and his son-in-law William Almy were among those who realized that to a young country economic independence was a corollary to political autonomy. With a combination of patriotism, self-interest, and mechanical woolly-mindedness, they had been engaged in several basement experiments with imperfect American versions of such machines as a stocking knitter, a wool spinner, a carding machine, and cotton-spinning frames turned laboriously by hand.

Obtaining their financial backing, Slater also had the good fortune to find a mechanic whose genius equaled his own powers of memory. David Wilkinson of Pawtucket, who was to become Slater's brother-in-law, was a blacksmith's son. He is credited with many sorts of inventions and inventive improvements such as an early steamboat some sixteen years before Fulton, and the sliding lathe, a device that started the manufacture of machine tools. This invention was of such importance that John Quincy Adams, by an act of Congress, procured Wilkinson a grant of ten thousand dollars in recognition of this achievement—a little belatedly, to be sure, some fifty years after the lathe was patented.[*] Out of his blacksmith shop grew what can probably be considered America's first machine shop.

Slater and Wilkinson remembered, worked, and invented, producing this country's first successful waterpowered spinning frame.

Almy & Brown began spinning cotton yarn in an old fulling mill. In three years they erected their own factory, just in time to fully benefit from one of the most important inventions of the century. Eli Whitney's cotton gin suddenly made possible the wide use of cotton at reasonable prices. Before that invention, cotton cleaning was a tedious hand job, the many seeds and dirt being difficult to remove. Like weaving at that time, cleaning had been "put out" in neighboring homes to be done by hand. The cotton gin changed all that.

When it came to building the mill, equipping it, and securing a work force, Slater in many ways depended on his own frame of reference—England.

As William Pierson describes in his unpublished thesis,[†] England had

---

[*] "The Beginnings of the Machine Age in New England: David Wilkinson of Pawtucket." Jonathan Thayer Lincoln, *New England Quarterly*, vol. 6 (1933), p. 716.

[†] William H. Pierson, "Industrial Architecture of the Berkshires." Dissertation presented to Yale University, May 1, 1949.

established a basic architectural vocabulary for the early textile mill, where silk-throwing mills and the principles of their design were carried over to the cotton industry. Functional requirements produced the basic form, unchanged in its essentials throughout eighteenth- and nineteenth-century mill building: a rectangular edifice, somewhat long and narrow in its proportions, with several stories, many windows, and an unbroken, uncomplicated interior space. Such proportions were adapted to the arrangement of machines and to the vertical transmission of power from huge wheels or turbines to gears and shafts or belts. The use of wood in shafts in the early mills determined how large the building could be.

It is difficult to recognize the original little wooden mill in the Old Slater Mill Textile Museum as it stands now. Additions and alterations have entirely changed it from a small rectangle to a large T-shape. In construction it differed little from a barn or gristmill with its solid wood frame. It was functional, sturdy, and tasteful, in no way revolutionary, with even a touch of the ecclesiastical in the belfry, clearly a reflection of the men who built it.

Although Almy, Brown, and Slater had some initial difficulty in marketing their American yarn, it began to sell, and, as the demand grew, so did the number of mill buildings.

Slater's mill and Wilkinson's shop were the veritable training schools for the first generation of cotton spinners. Nowhere else was the information available. The more ambitious of their mechanics were tempted to set up shop for themselves. Mills first began to appear in the Pawtucket area, especially along the Blackstone River, and many fine ones can be seen there today.

The Embargo Act of 1807, which cut off the flow of English goods, was a great spur to the nascent industry. These early mills call to mind the simple architectural forms of the barn and, especially, of the meetinghouse, with its many large windows and bell cupola. One unusual feature, which can be seen in the drawing of Slater's first mill, was the attic story lighting device called the trap door* or eyebrow† monitor. It slightly resembles a long, thin dormer, and admitted light through the pitched roof. Although wooden mills were built for many years, stone masonry had the definite advantage of being less combustible, and it was widely adopted very early in Rhode Island.

It was not long before spinning mills began to lose their domestic scale. As they grew longer and higher, they looked less and less like the familiar gristmill. The trap-door monitor was modified into the eye-catching clerestory monitor. The result was an intriguing silhouette caused by the extension of the row of roof windows clear to the corners of the building, giving a broken or raised uproof line. This was a way of admitting more light than was possible with the

---

* Henry Russell Hitchcock, *Rhode Island Architecture*. Cambridge, Massachusetts: M.I.T. Press, 1968.
† Pierson, op. cit.

trap-door monitor. A narrower but more usable interior space was created as well. There are examples of both monitor styles appearing on one building, as with the Carolina mill in Rhode Island. In some cases, a double clerestory monitor was used, as at Phenix, Rhode Island.

The clerestory monitor was very popular, and it became one of the outstanding features of mills from the first half of the nineteenth century. The one-company town of Whitinsville, Massachusetts, on the Blackstone River, has two examples of this kind of building. The granite cotton mill has a combination of monitor and dormer; the little red mill, an unusual survival of an early brick construction with monitor, was placed on the spot where the huge Whitin Machine Works began as a blacksmith shop.

Another early development came when it was discovered that there were advantages to removing the stairway to an exterior tower. This freed more space for the machines inside and provided some protection and escape from fire, especially when doors to the tower existed on each floor. It is difficult to say exactly when the bell cupola joined the stair tower, probably around 1814. This combination remained the sine qua non of mill building all during the eighteenth and nineteenth centuries. A pure and beautiful example of all these features can be seen today in the sister mills at North Uxbridge, Massachusetts. The Crown & Eagle cotton mills were built between 1825 and 1829 of expertly hewn granite. They are arranged in a remarkably formal landscaping plan, with the Mumford River running between them and two parallel canals powering each mill. The brick span that joins the mills is from 1851 and was added when they were bought by the Whitin family, who manufactured cotton as well as textile machinery. The clerestory monitor and the bell tower[*] stand out as the most interesting features. The mills, including a handsome brick overseer's house, and the fine brick and granite lintel machine shop and office have come to the attention of several national and local preservation societies whose hope it is to usefully preserve them.

By 1810 there was an astonishing number of New England cotton mills already in existence. Although no exact count can be quoted, it would be safe to estimate a figure near the one hundred mark. Preelectric lighting and heating systems and the highly flammable nature of cotton were causing great concern over fires. Pierson[†] tells the story of one resourceful millowner, plagued equally by the threat of fire to his holdings and by the exorbitant costs of fire insurance. Zachariah Allen capitalized on several ingenious devices designed to combat both problems. Allen is considered the father of slow-burning construction, although it is perhaps not entirely his own invention. His mill, built in Centerdale, Rhode Island, in 1822, had an outside stair tower with heavy doors, a

---

[*] When the authors visited Crown & Eagle in 1970, they investigated, with some risk to life and limb, the legend that the bell was made by Paul Revere. Unfortunately, only a German name was found.

[†] Pierson, op. cit.

▶

Mills along the Blackstone River.
Photo Courtesy New York Public Library Picture Collection

EARLY AMERICAN MILLS

Left: The Butterfly mill, Lincoln, Rhode Island. This beautiful granite mill of 1813 has none of the distinguishing mill features except perhaps its length. It almost looks like a Shaker building or meetinghouse and would make a beautiful home.

Photo Courtesy Joseph McCarthy for the Nickerson Architectural Collection at Providence, Rhode Island, Public Library

Below: Hope, Rhode Island. Different stages of mill building: (1) small shingled two-story mill from 1810 or 1815; (2) larger mill from approximately 1850; (3) with roof flattened at a later period.

Photo Courtesy Joseph McCarthy for the Nickerson Architectural Collection at Providence, Rhode Island, Public Library

The Freeman Manufacturing Company, North Adams, Massachusetts. This stone mill is one of the early cotton mills in the Adams valley. It is very reminiscent of the early Slater mills. Destroyed.

Photo Courtesy William Pierson, Berkshire Historical Society

Carolina mill, Carolina, Rhode Island. This small mill from 1841 uses combined materials of wood and stone. One curious feature is the combination clerestory and trap-door monitor. The building now is almost collapsed.

Photo Courtesy Joseph McCarthy for the Nickerson Architectural Collection at Providence, Rhode Island, Public Library

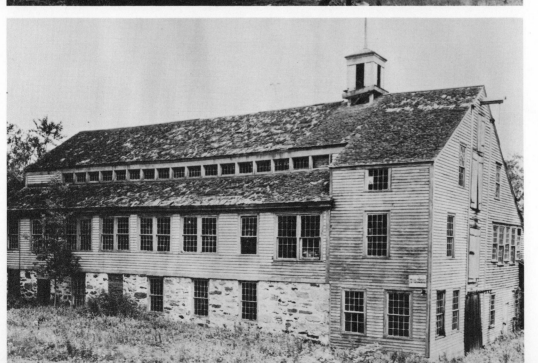

Davisville cotton mill, Davisville, Rhode Island. This mill of 1848 shows a closeness to domestic scale more typical of the earliest cotton mills. The wooden front part with its hoist could easily be taken for a gristmill. Another very old woolen mill existed here as well, but both were destroyed.

Photo Courtesy Joseph McCarthy for the Nickerson Architectural Collection, Providence, Rhode Island, Public Library

Above: Lippitt mill, Lippitt, Rhode Island. This early mill, from 1809, although made of wood, shows a development away from the domestic scale of the first cotton mill. It is the first known use of the clerestory monitor.

Photo Courtesy Joseph McCarthy for the Nickerson Architectural Collection, Providence, Rhode Island, Public Library

Left: The former Northbridge cotton mill in Whitinsville, Massachusetts, acquired in 1831 by the Whitins.

Photo Courtesy of Authors

The old machine shop in Whitinsville, Massachusetts. The Whitins built this little mill in 1826 to manufacture cotton yarn. It became a machine shop in the 1840s as the business of textile machinery grew. The Whitins acquired many cotton mills in the area, including the Crown & Eagle in North Uxbridge and the granite Northbridge cotton mill in Whitinsville, which so much resembles the Slatersville mill. The Whitins made their own textile machinery from the beginning in the old forge on the site of the brick mill. This branch of the industry far outstripped cotton manufacturing due to the invention by John Whitin of an excellent cotton picker in 1831.

Photo Courtesy of Authors

▶

Harrisville, Rhode Island. This impressive ruin is another Blackstone mill soon to disappear.

Photo Courtesy of Authors

Fred L. Sayles mill, Pascoag, Rhode Island. This is but one of approximately nineteen mills that once stood in the area of Pascoag, Rhode Island. Although the roof appears to have suffered flattening here, the mill cupola is remarkable for its frilly ornament. Destroyed.

Photo Courtesy Joseph McCarthy for the Nickerson Architectural Collection, Providence, Rhode Island, Public Library

Below: The Stamina mill, Forestdale, Rhode Island, on the Blackstone, is one of the rare few mills still turning out cloth.

Photo Courtesy of Authors

Above: The Sheffield worsted mill, Pascoag, Rhode Island, c. 1859. This woolen mill with steeplelike towers has been destroyed.

Photo Courtesy Joseph McCarthy for the Nickerson Architectural Collection, Providence, Rhode Island, Public Library

Slatersville cotton mill, Slatersville, Rhode Island. This is a rear view of one of Samuel Slater's first cotton mills. The masonry is reminiscent of England. It is in good condition.
Photo Courtesy of Authors

Early representation of the Crown & Eagle Mills, North Uxbridge, Massachusetts, showing the parklike layout.
Photo Courtesy Boston Athenaeum

Above: Crown & Eagle Mills, built between 1825 and 1829.
Photo Courtesy of Authors

Right: This photograph shows the rather formal layout of the Crown & Eagle Mills. Trees probably lined the canal on both sides at one time. It is in fair condition.

Photo Courtesy of Authors

124   EARLY AMERICAN MILLS

The Crown mill has the bell and stair tower. The Crown & Eagle Mills are said to be named for the mother country and the new country to which the builder had immigrated.

Photo Courtesy of Authors

Well-proportioned brick and granite lintel building for the machine and woodworking shops of Crown & Eagle. It is in good condition.
Photo Courtesy Randolph Langenbach, New England Textile Mill Survey, Smithsonian Institution

Above: Crown & Eagle. The bell that Paul Revere did *not* make.
Photo Courtesy of Authors

Right: Crown & Eagle. Water closet.
Photo Courtesy Randolph Langenbach, New England Textile Mill Survey, Smithsonian Institution

Crown & Eagle. Sluice gate control on canal.
Photo Courtesy of Authors

Below: Crown & Eagle. Elevation drawing showing the two mills, brick span, canals, and river.
Drawn by John L. Miller for New England Textile Mill Survey, Smithsonian Institution

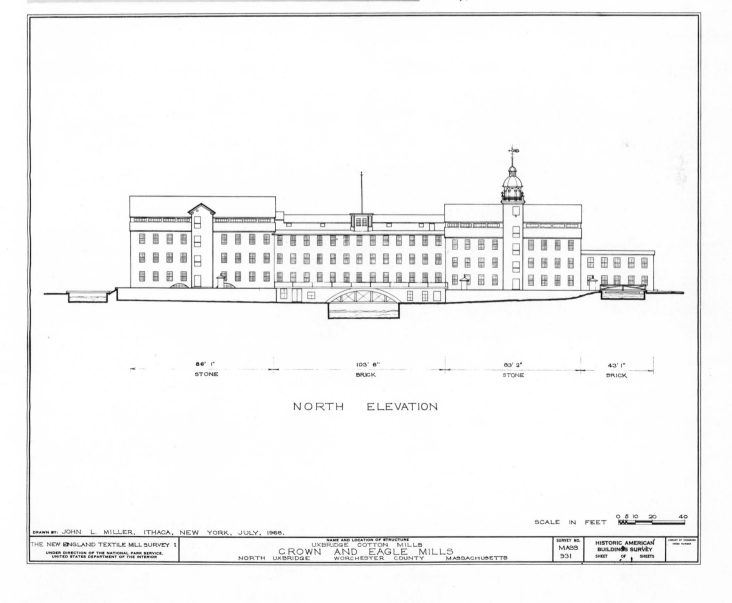

86' 1" STONE   103' 6" BRICK   83' 2" STONE   43' 1" BRICK

NORTH ELEVATION

SCALE IN FEET 0 5 10 20 40

DRAWN BY: JOHN L. MILLER, ITHACA, NEW YORK, JULY, 1968.

THE NEW ENGLAND TEXTILE MILL SURVEY I
UNDER DIRECTION OF THE NATIONAL PARK SERVICE.
UNITED STATES DEPARTMENT OF THE INTERIOR

NAME AND LOCATION OF STRUCTURE
UXBRIDGE COTTON MILLS
CROWN AND EAGLE MILLS
NORTH UXBRIDGE   WORCHESTER COUNTY   MASSACHUSETTS

SURVEY NO.
MASS
931

HISTORIC AMERICAN
BUILDINGS SURVEY
SHEET   OF   SHEETS

LIBRARY OF CONGRESS
INDEX NUMBER

Above: Crown & Eagle pay office. This woody interior still has notices for the workers posted around. In an old ledger one can trace a man's fortune. After deductions from the company store and for lodging, take-home pay was registered in the cents column only. *Photo Courtesy of Authors*

Left: An unusual sliding lathe in the machine shop of Crown & Eagle. It slides on a bed of hewn granite. The Smithsonian Institution has its eye on this machine. *Photo Courtesy of Authors*

▶

Insurance survey showing the plan of Crown & Eagle, excluding most of the housing. *Photo Courtesy National Museum of History and Technology, Smithsonian Institution*

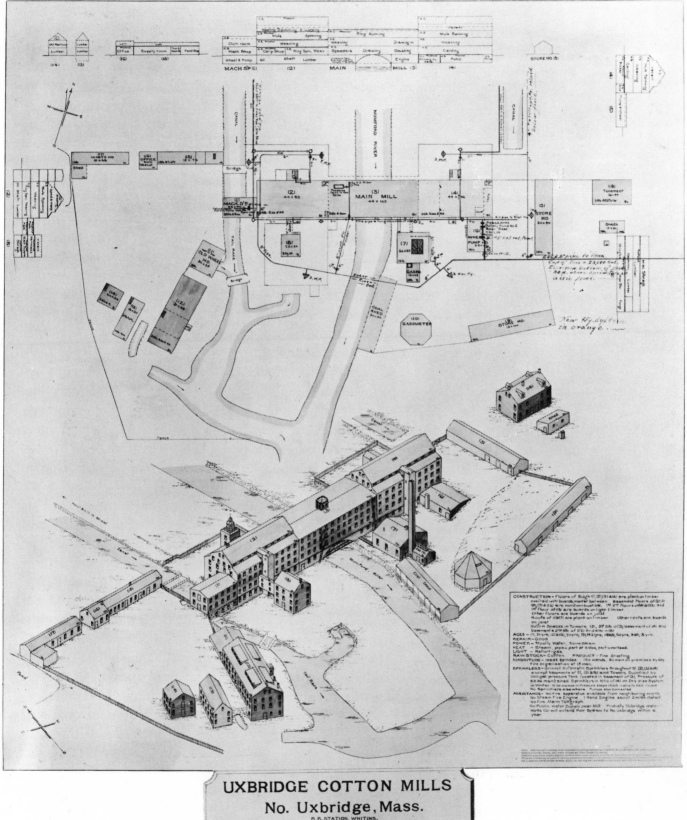

UXBRIDGE COTTON MILLS

No. Uxbridge, Mass.

R.R. STATION, WHITINS.

Surveyed, July, 25, 1892.

Scale of Plan 1 in = 40 Feet
Scale of view the same.

water tank in the cupola to supplement a hose and pump connected to his water-power system, and shingles laid in mortar and specially constructed floors. The usual design had been to set plank floors on a wooden frame of studs and joists. This design left many exposed wood surfaces and pockets of air, making perfect kindling. Allen eliminated the joists by using long and heavy traverse beams, three inches thick, with one inch thick floor planks directly on them. Surely it took some time to burn through four dense inches of wood.

When the authors were building a house on Cape Cod, they had the good fortune to obtain a used floor from a factory built around 1850. The enormous boards were three inches thick, eight inches wide, and twenty feet long, not to mention being cut from the center of the pine, the densest part. It was so strong that the subflooring could be eliminated, the old planks resting directly on the foundation girders. When our insurance man came to inspect, he confirmed our knowledge that such a floor was better than iron, which would melt to collapsing before ours would be consumed.

Apparently Zachariah Allen's insurance man was not so easily persuaded, for, with all the improvements, lower rates were still denied. Undaunted, Allen began his *own* insurance company around 1835, made up exclusively of other manufacturers committed to analyzing fire-prevention methods. From these beginnings grew the giant mutual, Manufacturers' Fire Insurance Company.*

Slow-burning construction was rapidly adopted by other mill builders, and it became standard by the 1850s. Unfortunately, as we shall see, the recommendations and requirements of insurance companies such as Allen's rigidified into a standard mill plan that had very little aesthetic appeal.

Mills increased in size as technological advances in the power systems proceeded. The turbine, with its belt system, or rope drive, came into use in the 1850s. Steam power was not used in America until over a half century after its discovery. For southern New England mills, waterpower continued to prove adequate into the 1870s. Although they reached the size of the Merino mill in Providence or the Allendale, Rhode Island, mill, their size was restricted to how much power could be generated from the stream, even with the more efficient turbine. Because rivers with the tremendous power of the Merrimack did not exist in the southern region, large concentrations of mills did not form. The mills may have grown larger, but they were still built singly as a general rule. Woonsocket, where most of the mills have been destroyed, was an exception.

The Greek Revival lent some of its decorative vocabulary to early mill building. It can be glimpsed in the wooden cupolas, in an occasional cornice, pilaster or pedimented form. The Greek Revival influence was slow in disappearing in the provincial areas of mill settlements, as can be seen in details of the Governor Harris mill of 1851 in Harrisville, Rhode Island, and in the mill at Quidnick in that state.

---

* Pierson, op. cit.

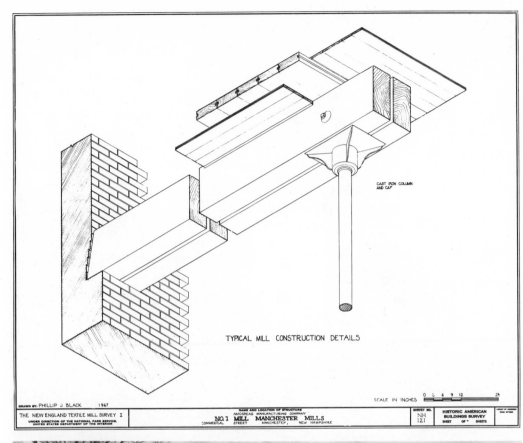

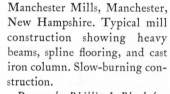

CAST IRON COLUMN
AND CAP

TYPICAL MILL CONSTRUCTION DETAILS

SCALE IN INCHES

DRAWN BY: PHILLIP J BLACK   1967

THE NEW ENGLAND TEXTILE MILL SURVEY I
UNDER DIRECTION OF THE NATIONAL PARK SERVICE,
UNITED STATES DEPARTMENT OF THE INTERIOR

NAME AND LOCATION OF STRUCTURE
AMOSKEAG MANUFACTURING COMPANY
NO. 1 MILL   MANCHESTER MILLS
COMMERCIAL   STREET   MANCHESTER,   NEW HAMPSHIRE

SURVEY NO.
NH
121

HISTORIC AMERICAN
BUILDINGS SURVEY
SHEET   OF   SHEETS

Manchester Mills, Manchester, New Hampshire. Typical mill construction showing heavy beams, spline flooring, and cast iron column. Slow-burning construction.

Drawn by Phillip J. Black for New England Textile Mill Survey, Smithsonian Institution

Cotton mill, Centerville, Rhode Island, 1863. Its original proportions have been distorted by the raising of the roof and the use of a different material for the addition. With a pitched roof, it must have been a striking mill. It is in poor condition.

Photo Courtesy Joseph McCarthy for the Nickerson Architectural Collection, Providence, Rhode Island, Public Library

Clinton mill, Woonsocket, Rhode Island. This mill is in the best Rhode Island tradition. It is the second-generation size.
Photo Courtesy Joseph McCarthy for the Nickerson Architectural Collection, Providence, Rhode Island, Public Library

Merino mill. This large stone mill with granite sills once stood in the Providence area. It was constructed in 1851, but has gone the way of most of Providence's textile mills.
Photo Courtesy Joseph McCarthy for the Nickerson Architectural Collection, Providence, Rhode Island, Public Library

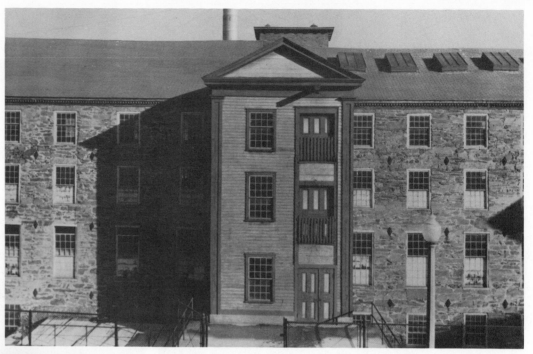

Above: Woonsocket, Rhode Island. Wooden Greek Revival proportions and details on a large granite mill of c. 1847.

Photo Courtesy Joseph McCarthy for the Nickerson Architectural Collection, Providence, Rhode Island, Public Library

Left: This massive stone mill of Quidnick, Rhode Island, has a long clerestory monitor that causes the eye to move rapidly along its length. It is considerably larger than the mills of twenty years earlier. This mill of 1848 is yet another example of masterful stone masonry that was not destined to survive.

Photo Courtesy Joseph McCarthy for the Nickerson Architectural Collection, Providence, Rhode Island, Public Library

Below: Governor Harris mill, Harrisville, Rhode Island. This granite mill from 1851 has Greek Revival details, especially in the cupola.

Photo Courtesy Joseph McCarthy for the Nickerson Architectural Collection, Providence, Rhode Island, Public Library

Mill building never gave way to the excesses of domestic architecture, neither in elevation nor ornament. Functional dictates were never entirely superseded even at the height of romantic vagaries. As Pierson points out, this is probably due to the fact that mill building remained largely in the hands of engineers or, at the most, "designers," and not of architects. Architects in nineteenth-century America were engaged in a bewildering series of revivals—Greek, Gothic, Romanesque, Italian Renaissance, French Second Empire, even Oriental Pagoda. Reflections of these can be found in the mills especially around the time of the Civil War.

Never was the mill builder so tempted to flights of fancy as when he contemplated building his monumental tower, as the combined stair and bell tower came to be known when it reached loftier proportions in the mills of the mid-century and after. The large tower was scaled to the increased mill proportions and continued to be as universally used as the stair tower in mills like the Crown & Eagle. The character, however, was entirely changed for now; in the spirit of Romanticism these imposing structures were awesome, threatening, dominating, inspiring, or a combination of such effects.

In general, the Gothic Revival called for forms too irregular or too complicated and too costly to find their way in the big mill rectangle. The Allendale, Rhode Island, mill, however, has unmistakable buttresses at the corners, and some millowners were tempted to fortify their towers with castlelike crenellations.

Right: Talbot mill, North Billerica, Massachusetts, built about 1857. It has a curious gothic arched bell cupola.
Photo Courtesy of Authors

Below: Lippitt woolen mill addition, Woonsocket, Rhode Island. This mill of 1871 is unique. Note the angle of its corners and the extremely heavy cornice. It anticipated the modern factory in that the windows are so large that only the small sections between them are used as walls.
Photo Courtesy Joseph McCarthy for the Nickerson Architectural Collection, Providence, Rhode Island, Public Library

Allendale mill, North Providence, Rhode Island. This large stone mill with unusual heavy buttresses at the corner and along the facade was built in 1822 by Zachariah Allen, the founder of a factory mutual insurance company and an early user of calico printing. The mill is in good condition and is still being used as a worsted mill.

Photo Courtesy Joseph McCarthy for the Nickerson Architectural Collection, Providence, Rhode Island, Public Library

The revival of French forms, such as the mansard roof, which harkened back to the Second Empire, provided a happy solution to the problem of roof line, as the mills grew too large for the clerestory monitor. Its curved line, usually with a row of dormers, gracefully accommodated a huge mass to the sky. The granite mill at Manchaug, Massachusetts, now being used for a chicken coop (an olfactory experience beyond description), shows a curious but not untypical blending of styles. The tower, with crenellations, a little rose window, and Romanesque arches, is joined to a mansard roof line. The Linwood mill near Whitinsville, Massachusetts, is a beautifully proportioned building. It has a mansard roof with true dormers and is unusual for the region as a brick structure. With its reflections of Bulfinch, it looks like Second Empire Harvard. It and the A. J. Sayles Company mill at Pascoag, Rhode Island, are complemented by offices that appear to be charming cottages, with patterned slate on their mansard roofs and bracketed cornices. One realizes the enormous scale to which all the details have been built only when the human figure is introduced.

One of the most beautiful examples of the mansard style is to be found outside New England at the vast Harmony mills complex in New York State. Here it seems no expense was spared in building that impressive monument to cotton and capitalism. One of Connecticut's largest and certainly most beautiful mills is the Ponemah mill of Taftville. From the water it suggests a French château. Its French and Italianate towers form a strange geometry in a clear fall light.

Old B.B.R. Knight woolen mill, Manchaug, Massachusetts, 1869. The Knight brothers of Providence in the second half of the nineteenth century acquired several failing mills in the Blackstone area. Their trademark was "Fruit of the Loom." This mill is now inhabited by thousands of chickens and will never be fit for anything else again.

Photo Courtesy of Authors

Linwood mill, Linwood, near Whitinsville, Massachusetts, 1870. Red brick.

Photo Courtesy of Authors

Spiral tower staircase.
Photo Courtesy of Authors

Interior view.
Photo Courtesy of Authors

▶

A. L. Sayles mill, Pascoag, Rhode Island, 1880. This mill is the last of at least six mills that operated in Pascoag on the Blackstone in former days. The present owner, Mr. Upton, manufactures cloth from synthetic fibers, but says it is difficult to keep going. He was kind enough to show us around the mill. *Photo Courtesy of Authors*

Above: A. L. Sayles mill, Pascoag, Rhode Island. This charming Victorian "cottage" is an office for the mill just behind it. Note the slate mansard roof and the ornamental ironwork over the dormers.

Photo Courtesy of Authors

Ponemah mills, Taftville, Connecticut. These magnificent mills were started by a Rhode Islander and reflect the mill pattern of that state, which Connecticut mills widely used. The mills began operating in 1871. Subscribers included several Slaters, W. F. Sayles of Pawtucket, and John C. Whitin of Whitinsville.* It is one of the most beautiful mills anywhere. The mill village includes many types of housing from various periods. Part of the property is being used by the fashion house of John Meyer of Norwich. Note the brick corbeling above the second-story windows, at the cornices of the building, and the belfry.

* Historic American Building Survey for Connecticut, No. 242.

Photo Courtesy of Authors

The revival that was perhaps best suited to mill building of the second half of the nineteenth century was the Lombard or Romanesque style. As more and more brick came to be used, it was found that Romanesque decorative motifs were particularly well realized in that medium. Even the plainer "insurance" mill often resorted to brick corbeling in the only attempt at adornment. Sometimes, as in the White Rock mill in White Rock, Rhode Island, brick was used in a strange but effective combination of Greek pilasters and pediments, Lombard corbeling, and Norman crenellations. Combinations of decorative elements from different styles were very common in all materials. The Maynard, Massachusetts, woolen mill, for example, has a Greek Revival belfry in wood on a brick building, adorned with Lombard corbeling.

In towns where a company prospered and continued to build mills and additions, a whole series of styles can be seen. In Whitinsville, where the machine works are still busy, an old engraving reveals one building with castle battlements and the one adjoining it with a Romanesque tower and windows. The building that ends with a three-sided apse needs only red Mediterranean tiles on the roof to recall an Italian monastery.

Where the single factory on the Rhode Island or southern New England pattern continued to be built after 1900, the revivals sometimes persisted. Thus, we find a few factories chronologically beyond the period covered by this study but nevertheless built in the old way. Such is the large stone mill at Sprague, Connecticut, rebuilt in 1905, and the brick American Optical Company mill of 1902 (see page 235), whose tower is remarkable.

Slater, his family, and colleagues were directly involved in mills in Rhode Island, Connecticut, and Massachusetts. Connecticut, particularly eastern Connecticut, followed Rhode Island's example. A considerable number of mills were built there, mostly in the last sixty years of the nineteenth century. Many single, large, and handsome mills are still in good condition in that state today. They are to be found in various parts of the state but primarily along the group of connecting rivers (the Quinebaug, Moosup, Shetucket and five mile rivers), which are tributaries to the Thames. These mills are essentially of the Rhode Island type. We have quickly sketched the architectural development of mills in the southern New England states, which can be considered largely the outgrowth of the Slater spinning mills.

It is impossible to ignore other important aspects—architectural, economic, and social—of the coming of the mills. Settlements of a unique kind grew up around them. Slater and his colleagues were directly responsible for establishing the mill village, which remained the dominant pattern in the region throughout the nineteenth century. The Waltham pattern, associated with eastern Massachusetts and the northern states, had a different village development, and will be discussed later.

Returning to Almy, Brown, and Slater, it will be recalled that securing a labor force was difficult in the face of prejudices against manufacturers and the

White Rock mill, White Rock, Rhode Island. This mill is a very fine example of ornamental brickwork. Note the corbeling, pilasters, crenellated tower, and stone windowsills. Although it was built in 1849, subsequent additions give it an 1870s character. This mill was acquired by B.B.R. Knight of Providence. *Photo Courtesy Westerly Public Library, Westerly, Rhode Island*

GROSVENOR-DALE CO.

Mills No 1 & No 2

NORTH GROSVENOR-DALE, CONN.

Above: Grosvenor-Dale Company, North Grosvenor-Dale, Connecticut. This large brick mill of 1872 is a product of the post–Civil War boom when more and more mills were constructed of brick. This one uses ornamental brickwork rather extensively, but is a sort of eerie place now that the landscaping has deteriorated. It is evident from the old engraving, which shows the boardinghouse and some tenements, that it did not always convey a gloomy feeling. It is in fair condition.

Photo Courtesy Smithsonian Institution

Right: This woolen mill in Maynard, Massachusetts, was built in 1848. It has a wooden Greek Revival clock tower on a brick building. *Photo Courtesy of Authors*

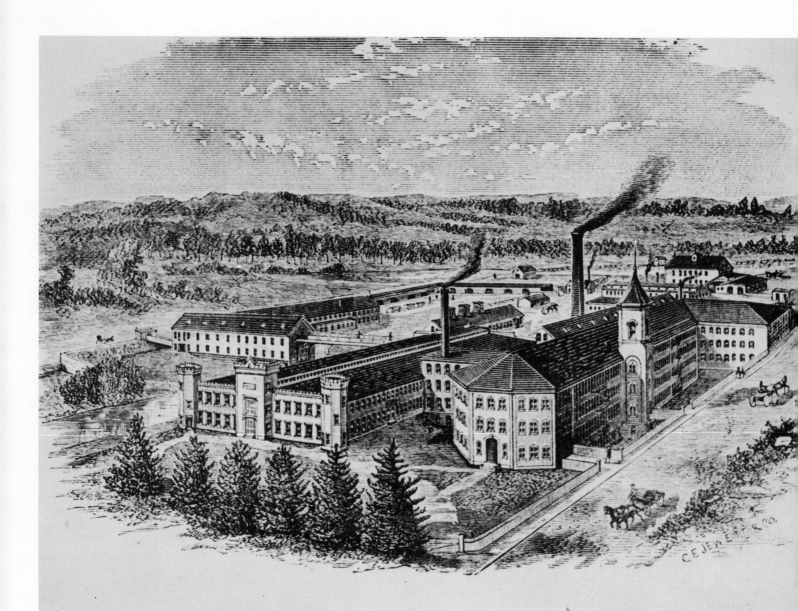

THE WHITIN MACHINE WORKS, WHITINSVILLE, MASS.

View of the Whitin Machine Works, Whitinsville, Massachusetts, showing a conglomeration of style. Note the "castle" and the "Italian monastery." *Photo Courtesy Whitin Machine Works*

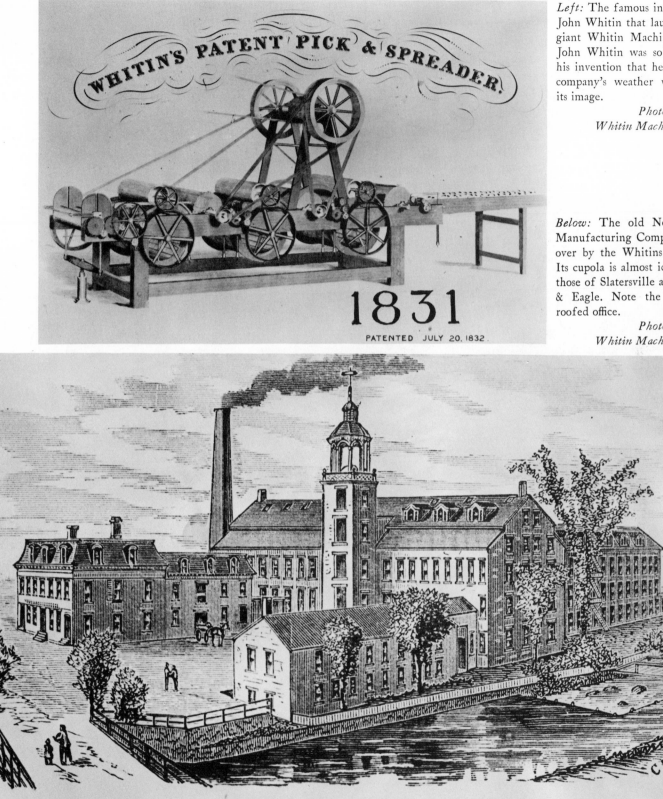

WHITIN'S PATENT PICK & SPREADER.

1831

PATENTED JULY 20, 1832.

Left: The famous invention of John Whitin that launched the giant Whitin Machine Works. John Whitin was so proud of his invention that he made the company's weather vane after its image.

Photo Courtesy Whitin Machine Works

Below: The old Northbridge Manufacturing Company taken over by the Whitins in 1831. Its cupola is almost identical to those of Slatersville and Crown & Eagle. Note the mansard-roofed office.

Photo Courtesy Whitin Machine Works

WHITINSVILLE COTTON MILLS, WHITINSVILLE, MASS.

Above: Famous Whitin textile machinery.

Photo Courtesy Lawrence Keeler of the Whitin family

Below: Baltic cotton mill, Baltic, Connecticut. This very large and imposing structure, begun by the Spragues of Rhode Island in the late 1850s, was in its time one
of the largest cotton mills in Connecticut. It is solidly built of cut stone with a
Romanesque tower. It is in good condition. *Photo Courtesy of Authors*

Willimantic Linen Company, Willimantic, Connecticut. This company, now the American Thread Company, was begun in 1854 for the manufacture of linen articles. The flax supply was almost immediately cut off by the Crimean War, at which time cotton was substituted. The company now consists of a series of buildings powerfully constructed out of local stone, dug from the riverbed. The complex is so large that photographs do not do justice to it. The engraving showing the central mill, built over a period of several years but begun in 1862, gives a somewhat better idea. Since the roof has never suffered flattening, the proportions of such a large mill are still very pleasing and the quality of the stone is very bright and fresh.

Photo Courtesy New York Public Library Picture Collection

competition from the ever-expanding western lands. Mills were built where waterpower was available, not where population was concentrated. Millowners were by necessity obliged to build dwellings for their workers in these ofttimes remote regions. They were also obliged to attract help by the amenities not only of the dwellings and their setting, but by the working conditions themselves. It is necessary to look into a few of the usual beliefs about life in the mill, beliefs that are based on what tragically occurred later, but which do not strictly apply to the early days. It is true that children were at first employed to run the machines, a job that did not require strength. It is also true that this system came to be severely abused. At the turn of the last century few children were educated into their teens, and rare, indeed, was the individual who was still in school in his twenties. It was much more common for children to receive schooling during certain months of the year when they were not needed for help in the fields and barns. Twelve or thirteen was the usual age for a youngster to be apprenticed to his future trade, and any schooling that came at that time was usually at the discretion of the man to whom he was apprenticed. In the context of the times, it was common to put young hands to work. At least in the mills, for the first time, children were paid for their labor. Slater and his partners must be credited with a certain sense of responsibility toward these young workers. The Sunday school was Slater's contribution to their education, for here they were taught the three Rs. It is not hard to imagine how much a ten-year-old child would relish a full dose of churchgoing, topped with lessons, on his day off. No one can consider this an ideal childhood. It was not unusual for parents to be employed as

Wauregan Mills, Wauregan, Connecticut. This is one of the larger cotton mills of the eastern Connecticut region that used the Quinebaug River at one time to power it. Its two towers carry different dates—1853 and 1859. It is built of local fieldstone, is much overgrown with ivy, and has a brick cornice and granite quoins. Some fabric manufacturing is still going on, but various other businesses use the building. The mill is in fair condition.
Photo Courtesy of Authors

◄
Willimantic Linen Company, Willimantic, Connecticut.
Photo Courtesy American Thread Company

their children's supervisors or overseers. Sometimes the employees were counted among those with a financial interest in the mill's success. A situation of cruel exploitation did not always result under such circumstances, and it is certain that the inordinate abuses of pauper and orphanage labor made life in the contemporary English mill of an altogether more purgatorial nature.

The early spinning-mill owners were anxious to hire whole families. They built their villages to attract large families. Throughout Rhode Island, Connecticut, and that part of Massachusetts that was oriented toward Providence, not Boston, in business matters, there sprang up planned, self-contained, and often remarkably appealing communities. The layout of a village usually followed a regular and simple street plan, with the mill as focal point. Because of its location on a stream, the setting was often very picturesque. A certain measure of self-sufficiency was necessary and desirable. The mill and cottages were sometimes joined by a boardinghouse, a church, a school or library, and the company store. When all these units were designed and functioned as a whole, there was much to be admired, especially from the perspective of a veteran of present-day urban-suburban sprawl. The rare village that is still largely intact presents an idyllic picture today. This is due as much to the appeal of the simple cottages as to the fact that the original planners were attentive to the part that space, air, privacy, light, and greenery play in the enjoyment of one's surroundings. The aerial view of Hampton, R.I., mill village reveals sizable garden plots for the use of the operatives. It was a direct policy in the early mill settlements to plant elms and shade trees along the streets and even in the mill yards. It was in the millhouses, or tenements, as they were called, that early attempts were made to deal with low cost housing for large groups of people and, in this way, they were innovative.

Although the reason most clearly was economy, the very simplicity of the dwellings adds to their appeal. The very first millhouses, those erected by Slater for his mill at Slatersville, Rhode Island, were built with a degree of attention to detail and ornament that was not attempted again. For the most part it is in the refinement of proportion and modest grace, rather than in an ornamental fanciness or pretentious scale, that the charm of these houses lies.

The early houses were mostly simple wood-frame structures of one, one and a half, or two stories. Some were double houses, some single family units. Although clapboard and shingles prevailed, there were, among the earliest, a few very austere and simple little stone dwellings in Fiskeville, Hope, and Georgiaville, Rhode Island. They seem to recall Europe of another age. It has been suggested* that the courtlike arrangement at Georgiaville is due to the British origin of the designer, the inhabitants, or both.

Samuel Green points out that the small one- and one-half-story cottage with a side entrance was rare outside of mill housing, as was the little trap-door monitor that admitted light to attic quarters. Both these details seem to have been well suited for use in this kind of housing and occur frequently.[†]

---

* Ibid.

† Ibid.

Harris, Rhode Island. Mill village street. This scene is typical of the best of the early Rhode Island villages. From what we can gather, the houses have disappeared; certainly the elms have.

Photo Courtesy Providence, Rhode Island, Public Library

Hampton, Rhode Island. Air view of Hampton mill village showing single- and double-monitor mills and a variety of well-spaced houses.

Photo Courtesy Joseph McCarthy for the Nickerson Architectural Collection, Providence, Rhode Island, Public Library

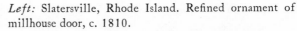

Left: Slatersville, Rhode Island. Refined ornament of millhouse door, c. 1810.

Photo Courtesy Joseph McCarthy for the Nickerson Architectural Collection, Providence, Rhode Island, Public Library

Below: Slatersville, Rhode Island. Later (c. 1845) and plainer millhouse doorway.

Photo Courtesy Joseph McCarthy for the Nickerson Architectural Collection, Providence, Rhode Island, Public Library

Above: Slatersville, Rhode Island. Slatersville mill housing from the 1820s as it appeared in the 1840s.

Photo Courtesy Joseph McCarthy for the Nickerson Architectural Collection, Providence, Rhode Island, Public Library

Right: Tiny mill cottage from 1810. Note the little monitor on the roof. A later, "flattened" mill in rear.

Photo Courtesy Joseph McCarthy for the Nickerson Architectural Collection, Providence, Rhode Island, Public Library

It is true that these houses were lacking in conveniences that our age requires: central heating, electricity, indoor plumbing, and the like, but they were not below the standard of the contemporary New England farmhouse for a family of the same earnings.

The early Rhode Island village set a pattern that continued to be carried out even into the 1870s and 1880s, long after the Waltham style began to decline.

The mill village remained conservative in its architecture, but there can be found some reflections of the bewildering sequence of revivals going on in patrician buildings. Undoubtedly Gothic gingerbread was too costly an affectation to be applied to factory workers' houses. Greek Revival details, though sparsely used, were so well adapted that they persisted long after their abandonment in the cities. The double houses at Hope, Rhode Island, are unusual for their mansard roofs, which are found more often in the mills themselves. In many places where mills were operating and expanding over a long period of time, successive building styles can be traced, or a variety of size combinations attempted. At Taftville, for example, the extensive village contains single, double, and row houses in various materials in street and courtyard arrangements.

Naturally the quality and amenity of mill communities varied to quite a

Georgiaville, Rhode Island. Workers' stone cottages of 1813–1825.

Photo Courtesy Joseph McCarthy for the Nickerson Architectural Collection, Providence, Rhode Island, Public Library

Hope, Rhode Island. Mansard-roofed cottages from around 1872.

Photo Courtesy Joseph McCarthy for the Nickerson Architectural Collection, Providence, Rhode Island, Public Library

Above: Ponemah Mills store, Taftville, Connecticut. This large square building with a mansard roof was at one time the company store for the Ponemah mill. The mill had its own dairy farm, which sold its products through this store.

Photo Courtesy of Authors

Pascoag, Rhode Island. Wooden row and double houses from 1845–1850. Note small monitors.

Photo Courtesy Joseph McCarthy for the Nickerson Architectural Collection, Providence, Rhode Island, Public Library

A fine clapboard boardinghouse at Quidnick, Rhode Island, as it appeared in 1940. Destroyed.

Photo Courtesy Joseph McCarthy for the Nickerson Architectural Collection, Providence, Rhode Island, Public Library

Phenix, Rhode Island. Mill from the 1880s;
houses from c. 1825.
*Photograph Courtesy Joseph McCarthy for the
Nickerson Architectural Collection, Providence,
Rhode Island, Public Library*

degree. As time went on and economic considerations were given more heed, human ones less, larger units were built, housing more people. Tighter spacing reduced green lawns and did away with picket fences. In the Phenix mill housing we see large houses crowded too closely together, wedged between a high hill and the mill, and ungraced by trees or grass plots. The feeling is claustrophobic; one imagines a life totally dominated by long hours of drudgery.

The best of the millhouses show not an architectural radicalism but something of an innovative approach to community and small-town planning. They are "a new combination and adaptation of existing features,"* well and tastefully suited to their purpose.

Henry Russell Hitchcock sees in the mill villages some examples to be learned from in our modern dilemma over mass housing. He compares them as a group to a typical modern housing development where the problem is "a cluster of superficially individualized though essentially identical houses, too many of one size and too near together to have much interest singly, too differentiated and too irregularly placed to have visually effective unity as a group."†

As the cotton industry began in the present century to desert the backwaters of New England for the South, the houses were sold off. Uniformity of maintenance was no longer possible, and, in most places, the grouping has been afflicted with cases of asphalt shingles or Day-Glo aluminum siding. So many

---

* Ibid.
† Hitchcock, op. cit., p. 40.

Sawyer woolen mills, Dover, New Hampshire. This comprehensive rendering of a middle-sized village shows two mills and their storehouses from the mid-1800s, spaced for water-sharing along a river. There is a pleasant row of operatives' houses set back from the street by green strips planted with trees. A boardinghouse and some overseers' cottages can be seen in the foreground, as well as the railroad track and station. Behind is a pleasant landscape of farms and orchards. It is clear from this and countless other artists' renderings of mills that they were not seen as a blot upon the landscape or as some social evil. They were sometimes painted from the same point of view as a farm or barn. *Photo Courtesy Merrimack Valley Textile Museum*

River Point, Rhode Island, mill village, as it appeared in 1940.
Photograph Courtesy Joseph McCarthy for the Nickerson Architectural Collection,
Providence, Rhode Island, Public Library

Cheshire mill, Harrisville, New Hampshire, showing well-proportioned brick addition very much in character with the rest of the town, if not with the mill.

Photo Courtesy of Authors

towns have abandoned themselves to disorderly and unsightly sprawl that it is difficult to find a nineteenth-century mill village free from twentieth-century blight. Yet such a town does survive. It is only a question of a few months since the looms there shut down forever. Harrisville, New Hampshire, has been called "a Williamsburg that's really lived in."* The mill, where woolen cloth was woven on antiquated machines, was forced to close in the fall of 1971. It is one of the marvels of the place that the Colony family managed to keep it going for so long.

It is hardly less than a miracle that the physical appearance of Harrisville has remained unchanged for so long, without the intrusion of a garage or a Laundromat to spoil its nineteenth-century unity. It would be a tragedy if, as the various properties are sold off, it should suffer the fate of most of our old towns. Harrisville is unique, the only unchanged nineteenth-century mill town left, and for that reason is an economic anachronism. It is a living museum of this country's industrial past—at its best. The townspeople are aware of this and have had Harrisville declared a historic district, creating a situation whereby any physical changes must be approved. Now the town has received a government grant—the first ever given to an entire town. Imaginative and farsighted planning is needed now to keep nineteenth-century Harrisville alive in the twentieth century.

---

*Peter Hillman, *The New York Times*, Sunday, March 28, 1971. "A 'Williamsburg' That's Really Lived In."

Looms suspended by the closing of the Cheshire mill.

Photo Courtesy of Authors

Harrisville, New Hampshire, mill of 1830. The cupola is like that of Cheshire's. Note the flying shuttle weather vane.

Photo Courtesy of Authors

It all began, as was so often the case, with a carding machine set up in the local gristmill. The first woolen mill, built in 1822, called the middle mill, ran for some thirty-five years and has since disappeared. It started the remote settlement as a manufacturing village. Milan Harris in 1830 built the simple brick upper mill, to which the stair and bell tower were added later. For 1830 it must have been an old-fashioned mill as a simple rectangle, shorter even than it is now. Although slow-burning construction was almost universally used by that time, the old barn floor framing was built and was not ever converted. The brick Harris boardinghouse was added around 1850. The various mellowed brick sorting and storage houses were added along the way. The granite Cheshire mill was begun in 1846, the work of a well-known stonecutter, Asa Greenwood,* who also had a part interest in it. It is in the style of other Rhode Island granite mills, such as those at Slatersville and North Uxbridge. The brick addition is of 1859–1860. This mill came into the Colony family in the mid-nineteenth century. Gradually the local store and various small buildings were bought up as well.

It is John Colony of the fourth generation who is now faced with the closing of the mill.

* John Borden Armstrong, *Factory Under the Elms: A History of Harrisville, New Hampshire, 1774–1969.* Cambridge, Massachusetts: M.I.T. Press, 1969, for the Merrimack Valley Textile Museum, p. 23.

Harrisville, New Hampshire. *From left to right*, Cyrus Harris—Henry Colony House, c. 1828; Harris Company boardinghouse; sorting and storehouses.
Photo Courtesy of Authors

Harrisville, New Hampshire. Cheshire mills boardinghouse as seen from the mill's roof.
Photo Courtesy of Authors

Harrisville, New Hampshire. Canal and storehouse.
Photo Courtesy of Authors

"Peanut Row" tenements facing a pond in Harrisville, New Hampshire. *Photo Courtesy of Authors*

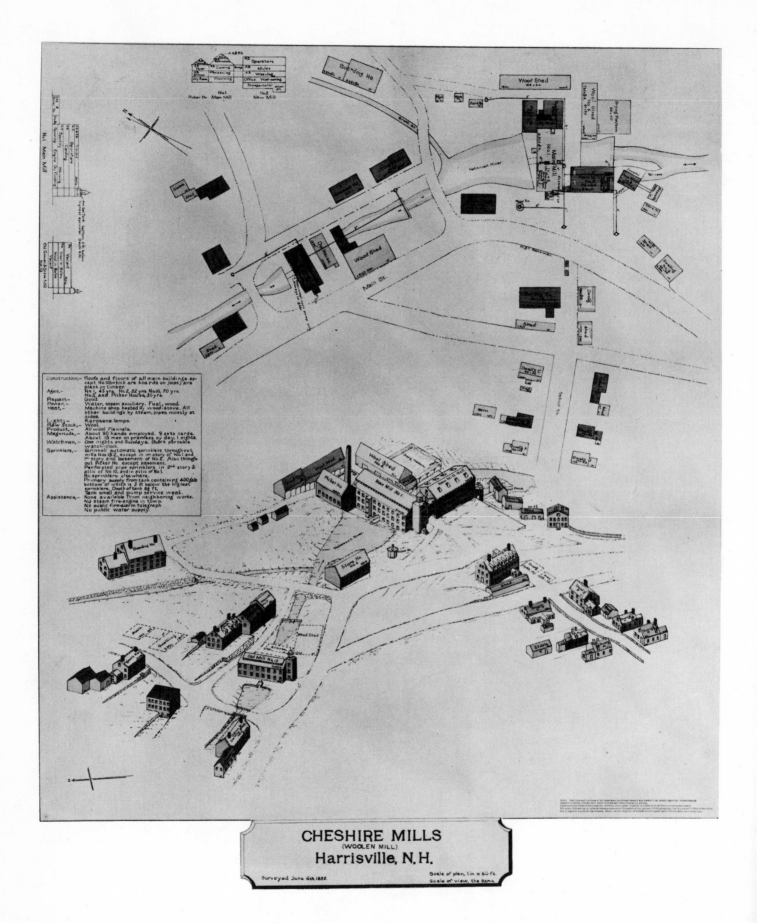

CHESHIRE MILLS
(WOOLEN MILL)
Harrisville, N.H.

Surveyed June 6th 1888.

Scale of plan, 1 in. = 60 ft.
Scale of view, the same.

Harrisville is not remarkable simply for its mills—finer ones exist elsewhere —nor simply because the town has never been changed. It is something *beautiful* that has never been changed. There is unity in the warm-colored brick used to build some of the houses of the Harrises and Colonys and the Cheshire Mills boardinghouse of 1850, as well as the buildings associated with the mills. These structures, with their granite sills and restrained proportions, are provincial reflections of Bulfinch. Both companies built wooden houses for their operatives with families and arranged them with great respect for the uneven terrain. It is a plan that avoids regimentation in the houses and in their setting so that ponds, streams, and the New Hampshire landscape are enjoyed by all.

Visually the mills do not dominate as at Phenix. It seems that the mill-workers at Harrisville have enjoyed the brighter side of paternalism in the policies of the Colonys. Relatively steady wages and employment were rare elsewhere in the textile business. The mills of Harrisville were small, the owners lived in the town, fully participating in its social life, working elbow to elbow with their employees in the mill. Armstrong points out that "it has been the policy of the Cheshire Mills for many years to do the major items of maintenance and repair on its tenements and to allow the tenants to deduct from their rent any expenditures they might make in improving their homes. It is also true that the company very often did not collect rents in bad times when its tenants were not working.*

The paternal system, which was the general rule in the early days of industry, is another curious survival in remote Harrisville. Paternalism was the natural expression of an age that produced many self-appointed moral watchdogs in walks of life not limited to the clergy. It was, after all, the age of the "white man's burden," when self-righteousness was supported by rationalizations of a deviousness equaled only in our own times. It was tempting for those in power to be self-serving in the name of God and patriotism, to practice a sort of voyeurism in the name of wise moral vigilance. As in all things, there were two sides of the story. A wise and benevolent paternalism, like a wise and benevolent monarchy, might be a good way to get things done. Under the paternal system, then, it was typical that a man lived in a company-owned house, bought goods from the company store, attended church built by the company, sometimes sent his children to the school provided or in some way supported by the factory. He would feel obliged to be mindful of his off-work behavior, language, and drinking. Life for the most part was scheduled by the factory bell, which told

---

*Armstrong, op. cit., p. 147.

◄

Insurance survey made in 1892 of the Cheshire mill, showing the irregular layout that is part of Harrisville's charm.
Photo Courtesy Merrimack Valley Textile Museum

The old company store of Slatersville, Rhode Island, is still standing. Slater's workers were paid in script redeemable at this store.

Photo Courtesy Joseph McCarthy for the Nickerson Architectural Collection, Providence, Rhode Island, Public Library

him when to rise, eat breakfast, be at the gate, start working, go home for lunch, start up again, and, at last, after an average day of twelve hours, when to stop work and go home. At worst, one lived under the tyranny of a petty dictator, with no job security, no health insurance or retirement plan, with no legal recourse when wronged, and likely to pile up debts in the only store where one's script was redeemable. At best, for those who sought that sort of security, there was a feeling of being well cared for.

In earlier times when labor was scarce and difficult to keep, abuses were not as likely to occur. There are examples at all periods of companies with a sense of responsibility. In Whitinsville, for example, when hard times hit, "make work" projects were created to maintain the population of that typical one-company town. The "great wall" of Whitinsville, six feet thick and six feet high, that cost the Whitin family thirteen thousand dollars in the depression of 1876–1878 is a monument to a policy of never letting a worker go hungry.* (At the same time there is no denying that it improved Whitin property.) Some companies were mindful that their workers got proper medical care. Many were careful in hard times to spread work among all employees, instead of laying off a portion of the oldest or slowest.

---

* Thomas R. Navin, *The Whitin Machine Works Since 1830*. Harvard Studies in Business History. Cambridge, Massachusetts: Harvard University Press, 1950.

It is still possible today to speak with old-timers in the small one-company towns about their youths spent in the mill. Louis Besettes of Pascoag, Rhode Island, and Chris Hedler of Taftville, Connecticut, both past seventy, seemed to have memories of good times. There was a feeling of community that both seemed to cherish, as well as a feeling of being looked after. When asked about the long hours, they substantiated our knowledge from reading that the pace of such long days was leisurely compared to the high pressure of later times. Mr. Hedler, of German descent, describes a sixty-hour week in which he "didn't get tired out," as witnessed by the fact that he was full able to partake in the many hours of dancing a young man might be required to do on a weekend. He remembers fondly a sizable community where Irish, French-Canadians, Poles, and Germans "got along and helped each other out," where a "good living" was $1.90 a day, enough for many to buy or build the comfortable houses of the village. He felt that his basic needs were taken care of and describes a life of occasional church picnics, boat rides on the river, and special times when the mill

Bell Time by Winslow Homer showing factory workers with their lunch pails—young, old, male, female.
Photo Courtesy Merrimack Valley Textile Museum

closed for circus day. It was interesting to hear of these things; they helped to dispel the picture of universal gloom, exploitation, and social debasement with which we came to the subject.

While the pattern of small factory towns, which we have tried to characterize, was evolving along its own distinct architectural, economic, and social lines, a venture was under way along the Merrimack River that became a prototype of American big business. It is easy enough, looking at a North Uxbridge or a Manchaug, to picture life there in the heyday of the cotton industry. But looking at the urban wastelands of such places as Lowell and Lawrence and Holyoke, Massachusetts, or Manchester, New Hampshire, who would guess that such disaster areas were once described as industrial utopias? A place such as Lowell, now associated with a grimness fit for the pen of Dickens, was, indeed, described by him in complimentary terms. Lowell, in particular, was at one time a "must" for visitors and foreign tourists, whose sometimes glowing reports on enlightened American industrialism leave us amazed.

The beginnings of the large textile cities must be traced to yet another stunning feat of memory. Francis Cabot Lowell, a wealthy Boston merchant with interests also in banking and other businesses, while on a rest cure in England and Scotland in 1810 visited the great mills of Lancashire. In the industrial city of Manchester, Lowell, probably considered a future importer, was permitted to observe the power looms where great quantities of cloth were being woven by totally mechanical methods. It must be remembered that the English vigilantly guarded the secrets of these inventions in an effort to maintain her markets for cloth in her former colony and around the world. Only cotton yarn was being manufactured under the Slater-Arkwright system in America. If the spinning mills dealt in cloth at all, it was only by the system of "putting out" their yarn into the homes of weavers where the handloom was used. Slater and others followed this practice and had endless bookkeeping and distribution difficulties as a consequence.

Lowell must have been a remarkable man to digest the technical information to later re-create these machines. "In piracy of this kind, so monumental that it takes on the character of a patriotic act, there was needed not only the power to dissimulate, but also a gift for observation, a grasp of mechanical principles, and a training in mathematics."* Lowell was also astute enough to begin to despair of the future of American shipping. The embargo of 1807, a boon to cotton spinning, was ruinous to many a merchant. Conditions in the endlessly warring European states were not conducive to the free flow of goods. Lowell's fears were borne out soon after his return in 1812, as war with Britain broke out.

Lowell was fortunate in his choice of a skilled mechanic. Paul Moody was to him what Wilkinson was to Slater. In the process of re-creating English

---

* Hannah Josephson, *The Golden Threads: New England's Mill Girls and Magnates*. New York: Russell and Russell, 1940, reissued 1967, p. 19.

machinery they came up with some innovations and improvements of their own. Lowell secured the collaboration of Nathan Appleton and Patrick Tracy Jackson, two wealthy Boston businessmen, related to him by blood or marriage, who were also beginning to look for new areas in which to invest their accumulated wealth.

From the very beginning, with the first factory of 1814 in Waltham, outside Boston, Lowell had a far more encompassing vision of what he wanted to achieve than had any man in the cotton business before him. With the enormous success of the Waltham mills, plans were formulated to launch a large-scale venture using the same principles. Although Lowell did not live to see the town bearing his name come to life and prosper, its plan was considered a realization of his guiding ideas.* What were some of these ideas? In comparison to the small spinning mills of the Rhode Island type, the financial organization was much closer to the modern corporation, granted that the shareholders were all "in the family." In the small individual cotton mills, partnerships were typical. These were usually made up of men directly involved in the mechanics and processes of spinning itself. In those days they were men not ashamed to be found in their shirt-sleeves, if necessary, working out technical difficulties. Customarily these men lived in their own towns. Their mills were not backed by great amounts of capital and were quite vulnerable to the fluctuations of the market. Lowell and his associates, on the other hand, can be compared to present-day executives, shrewd and bold money men, expert in delegating authority. It was their innovation to set up the semi-independent agent house to specialize in marketing, distribution, and collecting. They left highly technical matters in the hands of those best able to deal with them. They continued to live in Boston, busy with all their other ventures as well, seeing to it that capable younger members or newer members of the clan would live in the new town to look after their interests. Their talents were many, but among the greatest were their executive abilities and business acumen. Backed by great sums of capital, these entrepreneurs were able to envisage a much more encompassing form of mass production than people like Slater. They selected a site with enormous power reserves expressly for future expansion and hired the talented engineer Kirk Boot to work out a plan for the complex of mills at Lowell in 1820. It was larger than anything yet attempted in America. By analyzing the market, they determined that in the large-scale production of the cheapest and coarsest shirting and sheeting lay their best chance. The ever-expanding frontier gobbled up these sturdy goods insatiably. Fancy goods were woven in England on a scale and with an advanced technology with which they could not compete. Domestic production of fancy goods was centered on Philadelphia, where skilled immigrants had congregated but were still bound to laborious processes incompatible with mass production. Lowell's idea was to market cheap goods at volume sales.

---

*Ibid., for a full description of the business aspects of Lowell. John Coolidge, *Mill and Mansion: A Study of Architecture and Society in Lowell, Massachusetts, 1820–1865*. New York: Russell and Russell, 1967, for a discussion of Lowell's physical development.

The Waltham factory was the first building to incorporate all the processes, from raw cotton to woven fabric, under one roof. Even in Britain, sorting and picking were relegated to different types of buildings. This modern notion of the factory was continued at Lowell.

The Boston Associates, as the clique of investors came to be known, approached the labor situation in a radical way. In their eyes the "family" mill of the Rhode Island variety was not altogether satisfactory. The country as a whole in 1815 was still hostile to manufacturing, and the West offered the New England farmer a second chance and more hospitable land. At Waltham, Lowell and the associates sought to generate their large labor force from the one heretofore untapped source—the unmarried daughters of Yankee farmers, the very people whose hand-weaving skills were being replaced at the factory. There remained the task of convincing the fathers that they were not abandoning their daughters to a life of sin and degradation. High wages were paid, but, above all, close supervision was offered in company-owned and -operated boardinghouses, under the surveillance of irreproachable matrons. A rigorous code of behavior was well publicized. Girls were given a list of rules fit to prepare an aspirant for canonization. One of the attractions was the boardinghouse table, geared to satisfying appetites created by a twelve and one-half hour workday.

An exploitable proletariat did not exist in America in the early part of the nineteenth century, and stockholders could rationalize the merits of their system to flatter themselves. The fact remained that it was *necessary* to maintain a high standard to maintain a work force.

The girls came in great number, but usually stayed only a few years. Some came to earn dowries, some to send brothers through Harvard, others to escape a dull village or an unhappy home. Some came to buy fine clothes or join friends, others simply for adventure. Not a great many, it seems, were obliged to work because of need. "Far from belonging to a downtrodden class, the operatives who worked at Lowell and the other mill towns from 1814 to 1850 came from precisely the same stock, with the same traditions, as the overseers, agents and even the Boston investors themselves. Like the men who employed them, the girls were descendants of early settlers, the children of Revolutionary patriots, God-fearing and churchgoing, hard-working and passionately eager for education."[*] It is astonishing to us today to think that a well-bred, ambitious, and intelligent young woman would leave home for the factory town for an education and self-improvement. This is indeed what occurred. Lowell gained a reputation as a center of intellectual activity. In spite of the long workday, the girls made time to form "improvement circles," usually under the guidance of a man of the cloth, from which sprang the famous literary magazine *The Lowell Offering,* written and produced by the factory girls themselves. It astonished the world and was brandished like a Bible by the proselytizers of industrialization. It even

---

[*] Josephson, op. cit., pp. 62–63.

found its way into the French Chambre des Députés.* Of course, the Boston Associates were inclined to let much of the praise for this phenomenon fall upon their shoulders. Yet their industrial utopia did not remain so when it was no longer *necessary* to maintain the trappings of virtue, adventure, and culture. After a relatively brief period of high wages, a humane pace of work, comfortable living conditions, and a stimulating intellectual climate, the situation began to degenerate.

Other cities had been set up on the pattern of Lowell, the most remarkable of which was Manchester, New Hampshire. The financial clique of Boston magnates, their sons, nephews, and sons-in-law had an enormous influence in the cotton industry due to a complicated system of interlocking and overlapping directorships, chairmanships of the board, agencies, treasuries, and so on in vast holdings that included Manchester, New Hampshire, Lawrence, Chicopee, and Taunton in Massachusetts, and York and Saco in Maine. Up until the 1860s "no textile center in the country could stand up to the combined strength of the Mills controlled by Nathan Appleton, Abbott Lawrence and their associates. Without exercising an absolute monopoly over the industry, they were stronger than all the rest combined."[†] It has been suggested[‡] that their unwise business practices, such as overproduction and draining off funds to award high dividends when machines needed updating, were responsible for the need to speed up the machines and depress wages to keep up with falling cotton prices. Competition from other mills must have been a factor. Whatever the reasons, conditions in the mills worsened; the looms were speeded up, the price paid for piecework fell, the girls were given more looms to watch. The increase in stress and strain was considerable. This situation was allowed to come about and to worsen as the first waves of destitute immigrants, mostly Irish, began to arrive in the late 1840s. Here, then, was a ready-made "proletariat," with no farms to go home to when sick or tired, no standards to flatter, not demanding education and stimulation, and, above all, willing to accept low wages. They became a permanent laboring class. As the boardinghouse system decayed, as the speedup worsened, with no wage raises in sight, the Yankee girls could choose not to put up with it. Irresponsible profiteering was unleashed, and the dark age of American labor exploitation began. The potential for widening gaps in the social strata was there in the Boston system from its beginning. The men at the top were removed from any direct contact with their employees, who could hardly seek redress of wrongs from a depersonalized corporation. There was an entirely different relationship of millowner and employee from that found in Harrisville or in other small mills of the Rhode Island type. "Now, the requirements of modern industry turned owner, manager, and worker into cogs

---

* Ibid., p. 185.
[†] Ibid., p. 207.
[‡] Ibid., p. 207–215.

and levers that operated a super-personal, a national manufacturing organization."* It was some time yet before labor unions would be organized.

The physical plan and growth of the towns and the evolution of the mills followed this decline from idealism to unbridled materialism, from a sense of proportion to unspeakable ugliness and sordidness. The story of the millworker can be read in the architecture.

These early cities had architectural beginnings as promising as their social beginnings. Lowell and Manchester, in particular, were towns planned and laid out with no small measure of taste and imagination. Experts disagree over which of the two cities was the greatest. Several studies exist on Lowell, which was the first large "factory city" (see Bibliography). Manchester, begun nearly twenty years later, is being studied by Randolph Langenbach, who has made an extraordinary visual record of that masterpiece on the Merrimack, which is no more. The plans of these cities were infinitely more complex than the one-mill village of the southern New England type. A complicated system of canals had to be dug and adequate plans made for future developments of the mills and the town. Little hamlets became cities of tens of thousands in the space of fifteen years. In Lawrence, Lowell, and Manchester, large properties were bought up, as well as all the water rights and millsites. The Amoskeag Manufacturing Company of Manchester acquired twenty-six thousand acres between Concord and Manchester.† The mills, of course, came first. In both places parks were laid out, one sizable one in Lowell, as many as six in Manchester, two with ponds.‡ The Amoskeag plan had specifications for churches and schools, libraries and public buildings, to be built in the future. In both towns many elms and shade trees were planted. Amoskeag's Elm Street was renowned for its mile-long "forest" of trees. The entire character of these towns must have changed by the loss of these elms. When Manchester was laid out in 1838, its exceptionally broad streets were placed parallel to the river. In Lowell a more irregular shape of town was created to fit into the big elbow of the Merrimack. Manchester was destined to have a more orderly sort of growth. In Lowell the parts of the town not given over to mills and boardinghouses grew sporadically due to the real-estate policy of the Merrimack Company, which held some of the best tracts of land, while a squeeze developed in the other parts, and then sold it all off after more than twenty years, "only because the immediate prospects of industrial expansion were even more attractive than the hope of future real estate profits."§

In Manchester there was a more conscious policy to control the shape and spacing of the town and to assure a uniformity of facade. Conditions for building

---

* Coolidge, op. cit., p. 16.

† George Waldo Browne, *The Amoskeag Manufacturing Company of Manchester, New Hampshire: A History*. Manchester, New Hampshire: printed and bound in the mills of the Amoskeag Manufacturing Company, 1915.

‡ Ibid., p. 63.

§ Coolidge, op. cit., p. 39.

Romantic view of early Lowell, Massachusetts, showing the small orderly mills with their genteel citizens.   *Photo Courtesy Merrimack Valley Textile Museum*

Elevation drawing of the monumental tower.
   Drawing by Phillip Black for New England Textile
   Mill Survey, Smithsonian Institution

◄

Amoskeag, Manchester, New Hampshire, monumental
tower, still standing.
   Photo Courtesy Randolph Langenbach for New England
   Textile Mill Survey, Smithsonian Institution

Orderly and shady street of Amoskeag Company houses
in the 1800s.
   Photo Courtesy Manchester Historical Association

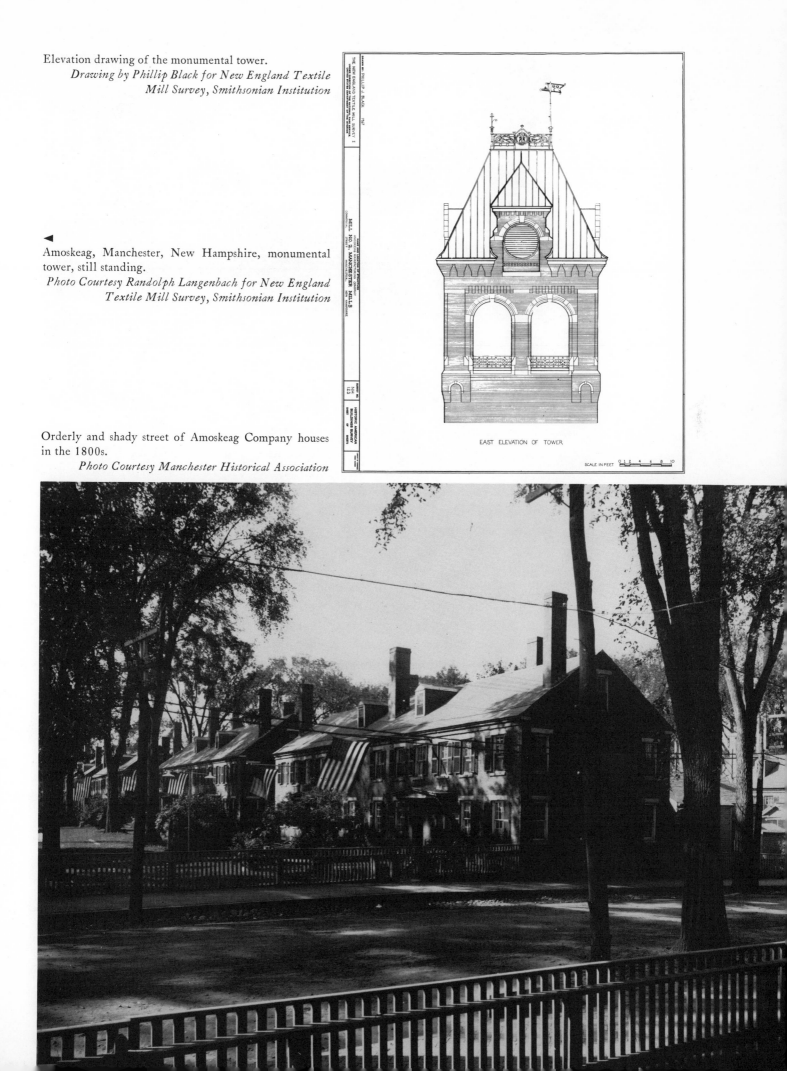

EAST ELEVATION OF TOWER

Manchester, New Hampshire,
row housing in 1971.
Photo Courtesy of Authors

were set before land was sold. "All the buildings on the West Side of Elm Street are to be of Brick or Stone and Slated. Every lot, large or small, will be sold with the restriction that for the space of twenty-five years from date of sale only one single building, whether store or dwelling house with its appurtenances, can be built thereon."* There was a special program to finance the building of appropriate dwellings by the operatives themselves, a plan that, to be sure, was beneficial to both parties.

Perhaps the most remarkable aspect of these towns, aside from planning, was the company housing, particularly the majestic rows of brick boardinghouses.

There is very little left to see in Lowell, but in Manchester, where thirty-five and one-half acres were covered by company housing, these beautiful rows can still be seen on the gentle slope up from the mills. Gone are the elms, and the houses are in such a state of neglect as to more resemble slums than model housing, but old photographs can bring them back to life. If such buildings were to be found today in New York City, only the richest would be living in them. One feature that is particularly arresting is the chimney line created by filling in the space between the two chimneys at each end of the house. It is this feature as well as the materials that recall the row houses and town houses of England. It was, however, a fairly brief period of glory.

As Coolidge points out, the social and architectural fate of Lowell was implied from the beginning. The Irish labor crews that had been called upon

---

* Browne, op. cit., p. 64.

Above: Lowell, Massachusetts. This old drawing from 1880 shows one of the later mills, the Appleton Company. The famous boardinghouses are seen in the background.

Photo Courtesy
Smithsonian Institution

Manchester, New Hampshire, row housing.

Photo Courtesy of Authors

Left: Manchester, New Hampshire. Helicopter view of the mills and housing of Amoskeag in 1967, showing mills, dwellings, canals, railroad facilities, and the curve of the Merrimack River.
Photo Courtesy Randolph Langenbach for New England Textile Mill Survey, Smithsonian Institution

►

Staircase of one of the Amoskeag mills in 1967.
Photo Courtesy Randolph Langenbach for New England Textile Mill Survey, Smithsonian Institution

to dig the canals and build the mill were not so thoughtfully provided for in the building plan. From the first, a slum area, New Dublin, existed, spread, and grew progressively worse. It was "one of the first signs of that social callousness which in a hundred years has allowed rural and urban slums to become the normal habitat of one-third of the nation. The tragedy of Lowell lay not so much in the horror of the initial situation, but in the fact that it grew progressively worse."*

It is impossible today to see the mills of Waltham and Lowell from which such things grew. Most have been torn down and those that remain have been entirely altered. While the typical southern New England mill was built of stone, wood, or combinations of the two, the brick mills of Waltham and then Lowell reflected the tastes of Bulfinchian Boston from whence came the entrepreneurs. At first the mills were quite small due to the fact that in 1814 at Waltham and in 1820 at Lowell the power system was still the pitch-back or overshot waterwheel and an arrangement of shafts. Certainly these mills no

---

*Coolidge, op. cit., p. 40.

Laconia, New Hampshire. Belknap and Busiel mills waiting for something as fine as themselves to be put up as urban renewal. *Photo Courtesy of Authors*

longer had the domestic character of the earliest ones. They were longer and several stories higher (than the original two or three), and after 1820 builders began to resort exclusively to the outside bell and stair tower and the clerestory monitor. It is possible today to see in the two old mills at Laconia, New Hampshire, something of what the Massachusetts mills were like. The materials are the same and the tower and monitor are there, but Lowell's mills were longer. The mills of the Merrimack Company were arranged in a quadrangle around a grassy plot planted with shrubs and elm trees, so that the whole resembled nothing so much as a college campus. Lowell was so much admired that its standards were imitated everywhere in northern New England, where brick came to be used almost exclusively. In Manchester, where all the bricks for the city were made eight miles upriver, the mill buildings were considerably larger, being erected at later dates. The unity of this enormous complex was largely due to the fact that when the Amoskeag Company sold land to other companies for mill building it did the construction work. Rare indeed is the town that can credit so much of its beauty to the work, either directly or by policy, of a single company. The solid mass of the buildings is given considerable grace by the curve they make in following the river.

Aesthetically the mills at Lowell began to degenerate when they were extended, losing the pleasant spacing between them that united the town with

EARLY AMERICAN MILLS

THE STARK MILLS.

MANCHESTER, N.H.

Stark Mills, one of the earliest mills in Manchester, New Hampshire. The Stark Manufacturing Company, reorganized, became the Amoskeag Manufacturing Company in 1838.
From J. D. Van Slyck, *New England Manufactures and Manufactories*, 2 vols., Boston, 1879.
Photo Courtesy Smithsonian Institution

Amoskeag, Manchester, New Hampshire. The graceful curves characterize the mills of this great textile city.

Photo Courtesy Randolph Langenbach for New England Textile Mill Survey, Smithsonian Institution

Amoskeag Company pay office in the counting-house.

Photo Courtesy Manchester Historical Association

the river. This occurred progressively until the uninterrupted masses created foreboding canyons far beyond a comfortable human scale.

The city of Lawrence was begun when the turn for the worse had been taken in Lowell. In 1845 the country was used to manufacturing, and immigration was beginning to supply labor of an altogether different sort from the Yankee farm girl. Lawrence became something of a boom town, and speculation aided poor planning in creating a situation far different from Lowell's in its beginning. While the joining of old mills was occurring elsewhere, the planners of Lawrence set right in to build huge blocks running along the river with boardinghouses set deep in their shadow. Building was rushed, poor materials were sometimes used, and several disasters occurred as a result: a dam broke in 1847, killing fifteen men, and an entire mill collapsed in 1860, killing and injuring hundreds. A scandal was created when it was uncovered that faulty construction had been pointed out by the engineer in charge and nothing had been done about it.

During the time that Lowell's mills were being joined, the monitor and double-pitched roofs were being flattened everywhere. The clerestory monitor, dormers, and other interesting features were eliminated. In the huge complexes on the Merrimack, the monotony of the buildings was certainly increased by this practice, and many a fine granite "southern" mill was spoiled as well.

AMOSKEAG
MACHINE AND LOCOMOTIVE WORKS.

Amoskeag machine and locomotive works and one of their products. Amoskeag began to manufacture locomotives in 1849. Magnificent ornate fire engines followed, and during the Civil War when cotton was scarce many Springfield rifles were made at Amoskeag. One thing that helped during the war was a large order from the United States government for four thousand dozen American flags. From *Bigelow's Annual Illustrated*, Vol. 6, Boston, 1857.
Photo Courtesy Smithsonian Institution

The canal building gate at Amoskeag Manufacturing Company. The company filled most of its own iron needs. *Photo Courtesy Randolph Langenbach for New England Textile Mill Survey, Smithsonian Institution*

The counting rooms at Amoskeag. This section of the mill complex shows the endless brick facade and the famous shade trees of Amoskeag about 1890. *From original photo, Division of Mechanical & Civil Engineering, United States National Museum, Washington, D.C., Smithsonian Institution*

Workers in Amoskeag's mill yard.
Photo Courtesy Merrimack Valley Textile Museum

►

Top: Pacific Mills at Lawrence, Massachusetts, now destroyed.

Bottom: Atlantic cotton mills, one of the enormous Lawrence mills.

From Benson J. Lossing, *American Centenary,*
Philadelphia, 1876.
Photo Courtesy Smithsonian Institution

Lawrence machine shop, Lawrence, Massachusetts.

Photo Courtesy Merrimack Valley Textile Museum

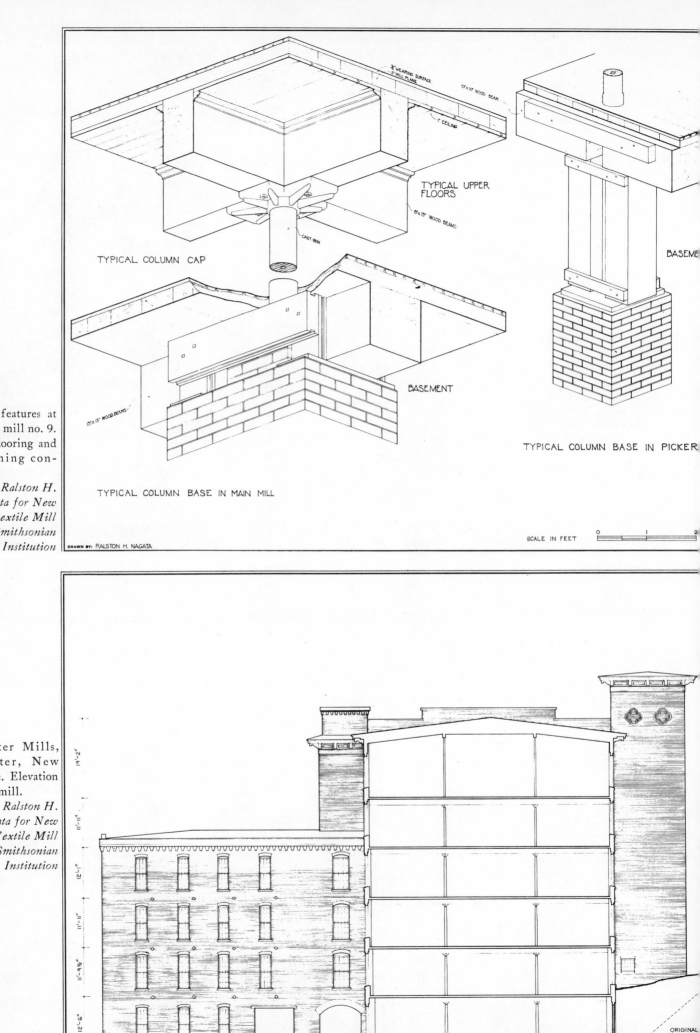

TYPICAL UPPER
FLOORS

TYPICAL COLUMN CAP

BASEMENT

TYPICAL COLUMN BASE IN MAIN MILL

BASEME

TYPICAL COLUMN BASE IN PICKER

Structural features at Amoskeag's mill no. 9. Note the flooring and slow-burning construction.
Drawn by Ralston H. Nagata for New England Textile Mill Survey, Smithsonian Institution

DRAWN BY: RALSTON H. NAGATA

SCALE IN FEET   0   1   2

Manchester Mills, Manchester, New Hampshire. Elevation of typical mill.
Drawn by Ralston H. Nagata for New England Textile Mill Survey, Smithsonian Institution

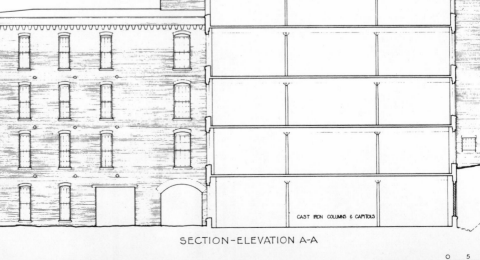

CAST IRON COLUMNS & CAPITOLS

SECTION-ELEVATION A-A

DRAWN BY: RALSTON H. NAGATA   1967

SCALE IN FEET   0   5   10   15   20

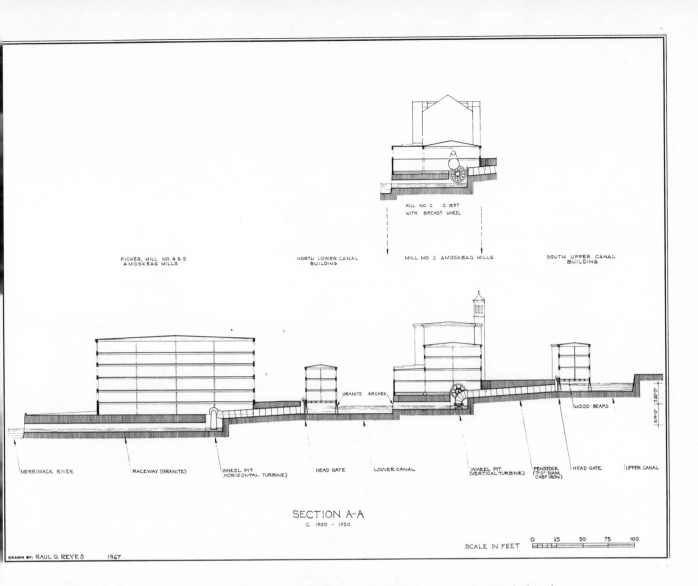

MILL NO. 2 C. 1857
WITH BREAST WHEEL

PICKER, MILL NO. 4 & 5
AMOSKEAG MILLS

NORTH LOWER CANAL
BUILDING

MILL NO. 2 AMOSKEAG MILLS

SOUTH UPPER CANAL
BUILDING

GRANITE ARCHES

WOOD BEAMS

MERRIMACK RIVER   RACEWAY (GRANITE)   WHEEL PIT (HORIZONTAL TURBINE)   HEAD GATE   LOWER CANAL   WHEEL PIT (VERTICAL TURBINE)   PENSTOCK (7'-0" DIAM. CAST IRON)   HEAD GATE   UPPER CANAL

SECTION A-A
C. 1900 - 1930

SCALE IN FEET   0   25   50   75   100

DRAWN BY: RAUL G. REYES   1967

Amoskeag, Manchester, New Hampshire. Cross section showing multiple use of water before its return to the river. Water was channeled off into the canal upstream. The amount of fall, or "head," between there and the point of return to the river was used to power several turbines. The drop in feet may not have been great, but the amount of pressure created by passage through the penstock and draft pipe was.

Drawn by Raul G. Reyes for New England Textile Mill Survey, Smithsonian Institution

In the meantime, the turbine and then steam power made huge mills practical.

Before the turbine, textile mills used large waterwheels, either pitch-back or overshot. These wheels did not usually make up part of the aesthetic of the mill because they were housed inside and were nearly out of sight.

When the turbine came into use, more power could be generated from the same water source, and a system of belts replaced the cumbersome shafts in transmission of power vertically from floor to floor and horizontally the length of the long mills. Much greater distances could be spanned without loss of power by the use of long leather belts. Very large mills could be built using this system. They sometimes contained several enormous turbines. With the coming of steam, it was no longer necessary to have a respectable spacing of mills, all sharing the waterpower. The coming of steam around the time of the Civil War was the ruin of the big mill towns. As coal was burned, the air became thick and grimy. Growth proceeded in a haphazard fashion, creating the hopelessly ugly crowding of an environment where machines and moneymaking left little room for man. Such places now are Holyoke, the Adams valley, Northampton, and other smaller towns where all sense of orderly growth is absent. These towns, particularly in western Massachusetts, had followed a combination of southern and northern trends. Early small mills, such as the old stone mill in Adams, gave way with the coming of steam to large brick "insurance" mills.

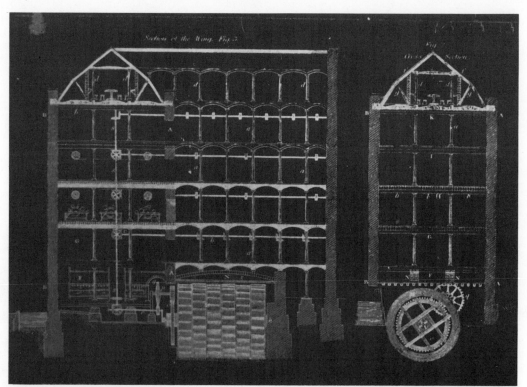

Cross section of a proposed addition to the Stevens mill in North Andover, Massachusetts, a plan that was never implemented, showing six waterwheels and systems of gears and shafts.
Drawn by A. G. Stevens in 1865. Photo Courtesy Merrimack Valley Textile Museum

Amoskeag, Manchester, New Hampshire. The dynamo room showing the drive system's hilts.
From original photo, c. 1890, Division of Mechanical & Civil Engineering, United States National Museum, Washington, D.C., Smithsonian Institution

Above: Looms in a weaver room around 1918 at Amoskeag. Note the enormous open space typical of the textile mill and the ample light admitted from the large windows. All these machines seem to be products of the Whitin textile machine works in Whitinsville, Massachusetts. Note the clusters of flying shuttles beside the looms. The clatter made by these machines all weaving at once was deafening. At its height Amoskeag turned out a mile of cloth a minute. At one time some fifteen thousand people were employed.

Photo Courtesy Library of Congress,
Carpenter Collection,
Smithsonian Institution

Brick supports for the now missing penstock that supplied water to the turbine of the Amoskeag Paper Company. Amoskeag had its own printshop where, among other things, a history of the company was printed and bound.

Photo Courtesy Randolph Langenbach for
New England Textile Mill Survey,
Smithsonian Institution

Above: Forlorn mill housing in Adams, Massachusetts.

Photo Courtesy of Authors

Right: Continental Mills, Lewiston, Maine. One of the octagonal towers. Note the different kinds of windows in the tower with its mansard roof. Now partly used as a shoe company.

Photo Courtesy of Authors

Since these were provincial towns, thinly settled when the mills came, housing had to be built. Brick row housing was the most characteristic development in these areas, usually combining the amenities of neither the double- or two-family house nor the boardinghouse. Pierson points to the sad fact that the bare and ugly rows in Adams crowd right down into the street for no good reason, cutting off the inhabitants of some of the finest mountain scenery in the region.* Maine saw a more important cotton trade than Vermont, which remained the least industrialized New England state. The Continental Mills in Lewiston is an impressive edifice with its block of ponderous square boardinghouses. The famous Pepperell sheeting went from Biddeford all around the world. The China trade of the 1850s to the 1880s included Burma, Ceylon, India, and Singapore.

---

* Pierson, op. cit., p. 238.

Above: Nostalgic packaging label for the Continental Mills.
Photo Courtesy Androscoggin Historical Society, Auburn, Maine

Elegant label showing now disappeared little office with tower in the same style as the mill. It must have been a gem.
Photo Courtesy Androscoggin Historical Society, Auburn, Maine

Advertisement for juvenile help at the Bates mill during the Civil War.
Photo Courtesy Androscoggin Historical Society, Auburn, Maine

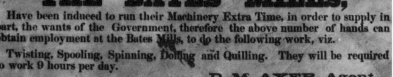

When steam came, the mills were crowded into the larger existing seacoast towns to make more use of immigrant labor and transportation. By this time the guidance of the insurance companies was responsible for the static utilitarian brick factory not worth saving. The steam-powered mills, creating dirty air wherever they went, were built in New London, Newburyport, and the romantic old whaling port of New Bedford, now consequently a prime candidate for drastic urban renewal. New Bedford and Fall River soared to their height after the Civil War, far outstripping Lowell and Manchester. In the chaos of Fall River, some handsome individual mills could be found, large of scale and constructed with great granite blocks. But it was no longer a question of town planning or elegant boardinghouses.

Pepperell Mills at Biddeford, Maine, whose famous quality sheeting crossed the oceans in the clipper ships of the China trade. The company was begun in 1848 and made army khaki in World War I. Now used as an electric blanket factory.

Photo Courtesy of Authors

192

Monument Mills, Housatonic, Massachusetts. Typical "insurance" mill, even better than average perhaps. This company manufactured blankets at one time. It is the typical unornamented big brick block of very uninspired proportions. *Photo Courtesy of Authors*

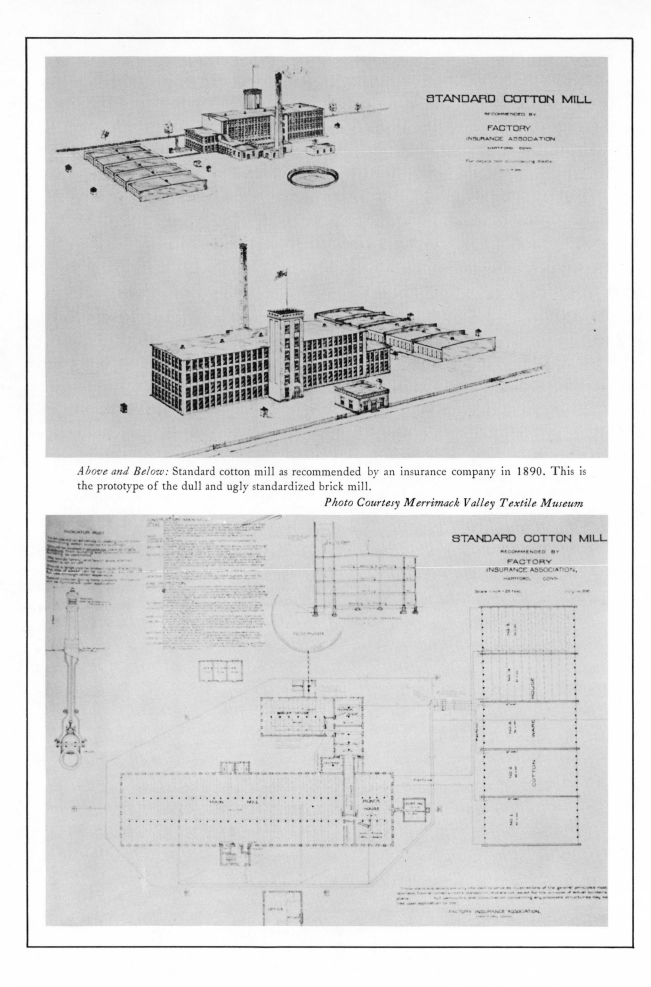

Above and Below: Standard cotton mill as recommended by an insurance company in 1890. This is the prototype of the dull and ugly standardized brick mill.

Photo Courtesy Merrimack Valley Textile Museum

The first mill of Fall River, Massachusetts, was a gristmill. It resembles early cotton mills. It has long since disappeared.
Photo Courtesy Fall River Historical Society

First cotton mill at Fall River, Massachusetts, now destroyed.
Photo Courtesy Fall River Historical Society

Typical granite cotton mills at Fall River.
From *Fall River and Its Industries.*
Photo Courtesy Fall River Historical Society

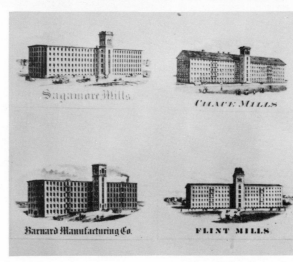

Above: Workers at Fall River.
Photo Courtesy Fall River Historical Society

Part of the enormous Merchants mill of 1867–1871 at Fall River.
Photo Courtesy Hine Collier Division of Prints and Photographs, Library of Congress, Smithsonian Institution

Chase mill of 1872 at Fall River.
Photo Courtesy Smithsonian Institution

Harmony Mills, Cohoes, New York. The fabulously elaborate mill no. 3 that was begun in 1866. While excavating for this mill a nearly complete mastodon's skeleton was unearthed and was removed to a museum in Albany. This is the most Victorian of all the mills. Note the chief stockholder, Mr. Harmony, in niche. *Photo Courtesy of Authors*

New England was not the only region of the Northeast to have large and spectacular mill developments. One of the most beautiful is the Harmony Mills of Cohoes, New York, near Albany. This large industrial town filled with Hudson Valley Victoriana is located at an impressive falls at a confluence of the Mohawk and Hudson rivers. This town of many factories had its heyday when the Erie and Champlain canals were busy with its many products. The Cohoes Company was founded in 1826 by a group of New York capitalists, including Stephen Van Rensselaer.

David Wilkinson, who so ably helped Slater begin the Pawtucket mill, was induced to come to Cohoes, where he ran the iron foundry and machine shop, producing, among other things, some forty pumps for the Cohoes Water Works.

Another Cohoes luminary was Henry Clay's protégé Canvass White, who helped engineer the Erie Canal and was an early proponent of hydraulic or waterproof cement. He laid out such a clever system of canals that water diverted from the river was used six times before being returned. This marvel was studied by various Europeans and even the Japanese. Today Cohoes attracts

Part of the Harmony Mills. Note deep mansard roof, quoins, and heavy cornice.
Photo Courtesy of Authors

Typical Cohoes De Chiricoesque millscape on a Sunday.
Photo Courtesy of Authors

The mansion, as typical of a mill town as the mill itself. This one belonged to Mr. Harmony and is now part of the Board of Education of Cohoes.   *Photo Courtesy of Authors*

engineers and engineering historians to study the remaining three of five enormous cast-iron Fourneyron turbines of the sort long since disappeared from places like Manchester.

A large hilly area overlooking the falls was filled up with company tenements ranging from single wooden houses to multifamily brick dwellings to long row houses. This area, numbering approximately seven hundred tenements, was a city unto itself with its own stores and police and fire departments.

The masterpiece of the complex was mill No. 3, with a statue of the chief stockholder, Mr. Harmony, in the niche. This monumental mill, with over ten thousand dollars worth of glass alone, was sold at auction in 1930 for a mere two thousand five hundred dollars. The mill stands a better chance of surviving today because of a carefully worked-out Model Cities program. When various groups of townspeople were organized to decide what to keep, rebuild, and destroy, it was recognized that the Harmony Mills, so important in the city's history, were beautiful and potentially useful.

Other areas of New York State saw some development of the cotton industry, particularly the Utica area. The town of New York Mills has what is believed to be the earliest cotton concern in the state, dating from 1827. The octagonal tower, topped with a dome somewhat reminiscent of Brunelleschi, is repeated in the two brick factories of the 1850s. The mill now used as the Utica Cutlery Company has some very fine brick tenements, some wooden row houses of a later date, and a pleasant elm-shaded mill yard. Like other mill towns in outlying areas, there is a combination of approaches to housing.

Cohoes Victoriana, a typical scene of the mill and mansion. The town of Cohoes has many mills.
Photo Courtesy of Authors

Part of the Harmony Mills at
Cohoes, built in 1866.
Photo Courtesy of Authors

Street of row houses in Cohoes,
their backs facing the falls.
Photo Courtesy of Authors

Below: Cohoes is the meeting
place of the Mohawk and Hudson rivers and of the Erie and
Champlain canals.
Photo Courtesy of Authors

New York Mills, New York. An old granite mill in bad repair.

Photo Courtesy of Authors

Below: Fancy ironwork at factory in New York Mills.

Photo Courtesy of Authors

WOOL

IN MANY WAYS THE WOOLEN INDUSTRY PARALLELED THE manufacture of cotton. It never developed into the gigantic industry that cotton became, and the technology of its machinery advanced at a slower pace. Mechanization followed a fairly consistent pattern of adaptation from cotton machines for use in wool. Architecturally, cotton led the way in developing the distinctive textile factory. The great centers along the Merrimack River, although they had some of their buildings used for woolen and worsted materials, were conceived as cotton ventures primarily.

Before cotton was much used in America, wool and linen were the traditional cloth fibers. Spinning and weaving were done at home by age-old methods, and finishing consisted of fulling, usually at the local fulling mill. Finer woolens were given additional finishing by skilled craftsmen. Napping consisted of raising a brushed surface with abrasive implements like hand cards. The nap was then sheared with large hand shears that required training and dexterity to manage. Before the machine age was much advanced, there were small shops with water-powered carding machines and a skilled cloth dresser or two. The cotton carding machine, first mechanized by Hargreaves, had been brought from England in 1794 by the Schofield brothers and was adapted to wool so that by the turn of the eighteenth century it was in wide use. Arthur Schofield also invented a wool-picking machine that fluffed up raw wool for carding.

Wool as an industry lagged approximately fifteen years behind cotton. It

Brick double house in New
York Mills.
  Photo Courtesy of Authors

Below: Pontoosuc woolen mill,
Southbridge, Massachusetts.
Old print of mill in its Vic-
torian stage.
  *Photo Courtesy Berkshire
  County Historical Society*

was not until nearly 1830 that most of the machinery to complete the cloth-making process was perfected.* The wool industry's version of the roving machine, called the Slubbing Billy, was refined by John Goulding to make a good even roving of carded wool. His "condenser" was not in use until the late 1820s and early 1830s.

The spinning machines followed a very complicated evolution from jennies to jacks to mules. The fully automatic mule was not in use until the mid-nineteenth century.[†]

Wool-weaving machinery followed Lowell's inventions for cotton. At first only plain, narrow fabrics were woven, but broadlooms came in around 1825.[‡]

Napping and shearing were wool processes only. A cylindrical power napper was invented around 1797, and a shearer called the wheel of knives, also cylindrical, became common by 1812.

The small carding shops gradually expanded to include a loom or two and perhaps a jack. They took commissions or orders for the work for which they had machines; for processes not mechanized, the work was "put out" to home industry.

Many of the early wool companies were established in Maine and Vermont, the coldest, most wool-wearing states. Very few of these are left, and even fewer are of any architectural interest.

The Slater-Arkwright system of cotton spinning was well under way, particularly along the Blackstone in Massachusetts and throughout Rhode Island by 1810, and by 1820 Francis Cabot Lowell's system for the manufacture of cotton cloth was ready to expand from Waltham to Lowell, Massachusetts. Wool lagged somewhat behind, but by 1830 factory-made wool was more common than homespun. The early wool factories followed Slater's building policies to attract workers. Pontoosuc Woolen, of 1825–1826, in Southbridge, Massachusetts, is one of the early full-fledged woolen factories. Its owners built a fair-sized mill village for the workers. The factory building is somewhat altered from its original state but is still very attractive. At one point it was lengthened and the slated Victorian tower was added. It must have resembled the early Lowell and Waltham mills or those at Laconia, being brick with a belfry and clerestory monitor.

Vermont had a considerable development in the woolen industry over a period of time. Some of the buildings are still used to make wool. The most

▶

The Pontoosuc Woolen Company is one of the earliest woolen factories. It dates from 1825–1826. This old photograph shows the tower that was added later. It is in fair condition. *Copy of an old photograph found in the building.*

* Arthur Harrison Cole, *The American Wool Manufacturer*. Cambridge, Massachusetts: Harvard University Press, 1926. See for complete discussion.
[†] Ibid., p. 114.
[‡] Ibid.

The Gaymont Woolen Company mill in Ludlow, Vermont, is now used by General Electric. It is one of Vermont's oldest and largest remaining woolen mills in an area where there once was a concentration of six woolen mills.

Photo Courtesy Vermont Development Commission, Montpelier, Vermont

interesting of the Vermont woolen mills that we photographed are from around the Civil War period when the "cotton famine" hit the North and wool was used for army uniforms. The area around Quechee, Vermont, was a thriving woolen center. The Dewey Mills, located in Quechee and towns around the area, have nearly all been destroyed, but one of them is being used in a most imaginative way, as a playhouse in the Quechee Lakes Development. Other woolen mills in the area are the old Murdock mill in Proctorsville and the handsome Gaymont Woolen Company mill in Ludlow, which is now being used by General Electric and is one of the nicest mills in the state.

The granite mill in Manchaug, Massachusetts, the chicken-coop mill mentioned earlier, was a woolen mill of the Rhode Island tradition. Harrisville, New Hampshire, is the jewel of the New England woolen industry, more for the entire complex than for the individual mills.

The later woolen mills in the large textile cities are virtually indistinguishable from the cotton mills around them and are seldom more appealing. The basic textile mill requirements were followed by both industries, but cotton, for the most part, produced the most interesting buildings.

China mill, Suncook, New Hampshire. This is the mill that at one time was proposed for a retirement community. Although not the most outstanding mill, its size and location near a town with lots of open space made such a project feasible.   *Photo Courtesy of Authors*

Ponemah mills, Taftville, Connecticut. These magnificent mills were started by a Rhode Islander and reflect the mill pattern of that state, which Connecticut mills widely used. The mills began operating in 1871. Subscribers included several Slaters, W. F. Sayles of Pawtucket, and John C. Whitin of Whitinsville.* It is one of the most beautiful mills anywhere. The mill village includes many types of housing from various periods. Part of the property is being used by the fashion house of John Meyer of Norwich. Note the brick corbeling above the second-story windows, at the cornices of the building, and the belfry.

* Historic American Building Survey for Connecticut, No. 242. *Photo Courtesy of Authors*

Pejepscot Paper Company, Brunswick, Maine, 1868.   *Photo Courtesy of Authors*

Old Murdock mill, in Proctorsville, Vermont, now in poor
condition.
Photo Courtesy of Authors

Dewey Mills, Quechee, Vermont. Destroyed.
Photo Courtesy Mr. Dewey.

Hillsboro, New Hampshire. The decaying knitting mill and its falls.

Photo Courtesy of Authors

This old woolen knitting mill in Hillsboro, New Hampshire, in serious disrepair, was begun on the site of a wool-carding operation in 1806. In 1828 a cotton wadding and bath company was begun, and the present factory, which made knitted woolen underwear and hosiery, was begun around 1865.

Photo Courtesy of Authors

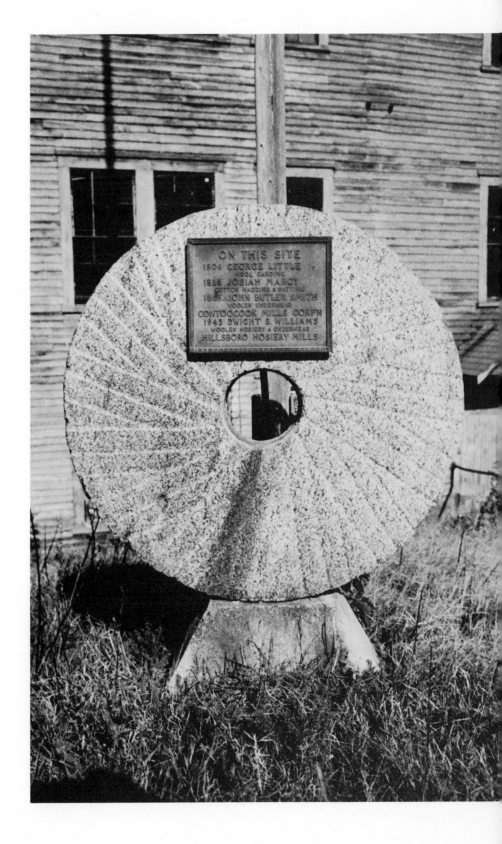

3

MISCELLANEOUS INDUSTRIES

CLOCKS

THE AREA JUST WEST OF HARTFORD, CONNECTICUT, became an early center of clockmaking in America. One of the very earliest uses of the principles of mass production was in the manufacture of clock parts. Eli Terry was the first man to test the system of interchangeable parts on clockworks that were cut from wood. He was mass-producing clocks using machine methods by 1809. Terry was a clever inventor. No sooner was one clock a great success than he discovered a new style or production method. At first he made tall grandfather clocks, but soon he found a way to make a mantel or shelf clock. Later he decided to try using mass-produced parts made from stamped brass instead of wood. This sturdier and unwarpable material was soon adopted by other clockmakers.

There is very little left of Terry's clock manufactory, only a broken-down waterwheel on a commercial strip of road in Terryville, Connecticut. Terry's son must have had the same penchant for intricate little machines, for he founded the James Terry & Company's Lock Manufactory in Terryville and found his final resting place right beside the factory. The area became a center of lock as well as clock manufacturing and, at one time, was full of early industrial buildings. It is not surprising to know that Eli Terry's business started out in an old gristmill at the turn of the eighteenth century. Early in his career, he hired a young carpenter to build his clock casings. Seth Thomas became a clockmaker in his own right, taking over Eli Terry's first factory as Terry expanded. Seth

Above: One of Eli Terry's early
wooden-works clocks now on display
at the Bristol Clock Museum, Bristol,
Connecticut.

Photo Courtesy of Authors

The remains of Eli Terry's waterwheel of 1824, in Terryville, Connecticut—all that is left of Terry's
Manufactory.

Photo Courtesy of Authors

LEWIS LOCK C?, TERRYVILLE.

Above and Right: Lewis Lock Company, Terryville, and James Terry & Company's Lock Manufactory, Terryville. These are two of the many clock and lock companies in the area of Thomaston, Bristol, and Terryville, Connecticut.

From a regional map on display
at the Bristol Clock Museum

JAMES TERRY & C?S LOCK MANUFACTORY, TERRYVILLE.

Thomas clocks are still being made (as a division of the General Time Corporation), and the whole village of Thomaston, Connecticut, grew up around the factory. Thomas, though a consummate craftsman, was not the clever inventor that Terry was and was always forced to follow Terry's lead in clockmaking styles or go out of business. He probably would have been content to stick with the tall and dignified pillar-and-scroll clocks, but, being a good businessman, he changed with the times and thrived.

At one point even Seth Thomas caught cotton mill fever. He built his mill in 1830 on the Naugatuck River and supplied his workers with low-cost housing near the factory. It seems to have been a fairly standard small cotton mill—five stories, with a bell tower and clerestory monitor. It was a great success until the Civil War cotton famine in the North. With no problem he converted the mill to a clock-movements shop and kept his workers busy.

This cotton mill built by Seth Thomas in 1830 was converted to a clock-movements factory when the Civil War cut off his cotton supply. It is very similar to the small Rhode Island mills of the first quarter of the nineteenth century. Destroyed.

Photo Courtesy General Time Corp., Seth Thomas Division, Thomaston, Connecticut

The business expanded to the production of alarm clocks, marine clocks, and countless other items, but the product that made Seth Thomas one of the best-known clockmakers in the country was the tower clock. This division was begun in 1872. These large clocks are still to be found everywhere—in railroad stations, schools, church and factory towers, and municipal buildings. The Seth Thomas Company made the centennial tower clock for Independence Hall in Philadelphia. The bell alone weighed thirteen thousand pounds.* Seth Thomas tower clocks traveled the world over—one reached Peru over the Andes by llama.†

The largest single-faced clock in the world sits on the Colgate building across from Manhattan in Jersey City, New Jersey. Another famous Seth Thomas clock is in the Grand Central Station tower. There is even a double-faced street clock on Fifth Avenue near 42nd Street.

---

* John R. Sangster, "Seth Thomas, a Yankee Clock Maker." *Bulletin of the National Association of Watch and Clock Collectors, Inc.*, vol. XIII, nos. 133, 135, 136.
† Ibid.

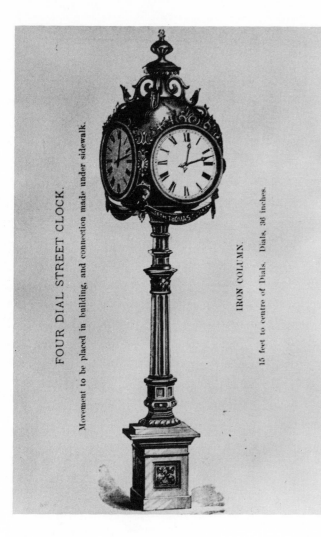

FOUR DIAL STREET CLOCK.

Movement to be placed in building, and connection made under sidewalk.

IRON COLUMN.

15 feet to centre of Dials. Dials, 30 inches.

Left and Below: Seth Thomas street clock and clock parts from an old Seth Thomas catalog in the possession of General Time Corp.

Photos Courtesy General Time Corp., Seth Thomas Division, Thomaston, Connecticut

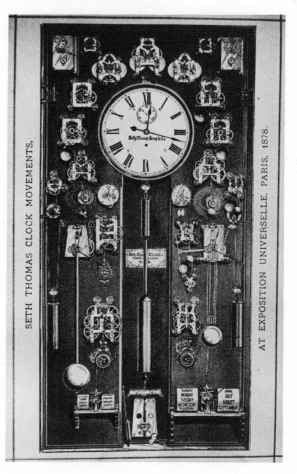

SETH THOMAS CLOCK MOVEMENTS.

AT EXPOSITION UNIVERSELLE, PARIS, 1878.

Arms for the world's largest clock, made for the Colgate Company by Seth Thomas.
Photo Courtesy General Time Corp., Seth Thomas Division, Thomaston, Connecticut

Workers sitting on the arm of the Colgate clock.
Photo Courtesy General Time Corp., Seth Thomas Division, Thomaston, Connecticut

EARLY AMERICAN MILLS

PAPER

PAPER, A PRODUCT OF VARIOUS CELLULOSE FIBERS obtained from cotton, wood, hemp, jute, seed flax, bagasse, and esparto, is thought to be an invention of the ancient Chinese. It gradually made its way west. The word "paper" comes from the Egyptian plant papyrus, which was used for writing. In Europe paper was first used for ecclesiastical texts, royal documents, and copies of the classics. It was first used for printing by Gutenberg, the inventor of movable type and printer of the magnificent Gutenberg Bible.

Paper was traditionally made by a tedious hand process. Even today very fine artists' papers are made that way, particularly in France, England, and Italy. Handmade papers are strong, durable, colorfast, and texturally beautiful. European papers are made from rags of cotton, linen, or a mixture of the two. Handmade Oriental papers are made directly from plants such as rice and use a great variety of textures, weights, transparencies, and patterns.

Papermaking in the West followed a complex procedure requiring skilled labor. Rags were macerated by hand or by an invention called the hollander, which consisted of a cylindrical vat with revolving knives that mashed the rags to a pulp. A mold or wooden frame with a close wire mesh was dipped into the pulp, removed, and then shaken to remove excess moisture and to cause the fibers of the layer of pulp to mesh and interlace. The mold was then turned upside-down and the sheet called a post fell out and was pressed between two felt blankets to squeeze out the remaining moisture. The amount of pressure applied is part of what distinguishes one paper from another. After a repeat of this process, the paper is hung up to dry. After drying, the paper is sized and glazed. European sizing is usually made from animal hides, bones, or hooves. If a glazed surface is required, the paper is run through smooth rollers.

The deckled or irregular edge is a mark of handmade paper. Most quality papers have a watermark embedded in them. It is formed by a pattern woven into the wire mesh of the mold and carries an identifying name, symbol, or emblem.

Machine-made wood-pulp papers are less durable and attractive than handmade or rag papers and they have a tendency to discolor with time. Wood pulp is the primary ingredient of most machine-made papers, although rags and old paper are also used. The first pulp mill in the United States was started in Stockbridge, Massachusetts, around the time of the Civil War by Albert Pagenstecher. The ingredients are beaten, mashed, and refined into a smelly mixture that includes sulfuric acid and a sizing such as resin, starch, and clay, which gives opacity and brightness to the paper. In the final process the pulp is diluted and rinsed with water and formed on an endless wire-mesh screen that shakes the fibers together. It is then pressed through felts.

In America the first papermaking establishment was begun in 1690 at Paper Mill Run, now a part of greater Philadelphia. It was begun by one William Bradford and William Rittinghuysen (Rittenhouse), a Dutch Mennonite preacher.

A second venture was begun in the same locality in 1710 by William De Wees and Thomas Willcox. Their Ivy Mills made paper for the new United States currency and for the publication of Benjamin Franklin's works. Other early mills were started in Alstead, New Hampshire; Bellows Falls, Vermont; Roslyn, Long Island; and Milton, Massachusetts. The first American papermaking machinery was constructed in 1816 by Thomas Gilpin near Wilmington, Delaware. It consisted of a revolving cylinder that dipped into the vat, gathering on its surface the mixture that, when dried, formed paper.

In our travels we found very few paper mills that were interesting from an architectural point of view. We were struck more by the ecological violence done by pulp mills. The old family-run company of Crane paper in Dalton, Massachusetts, has an interesting paper museum, The Old Stone Mill, set up in a building dating from 1844. The Crane Company was started in 1801 and has earned and retained a reputation for very fine papers. Among other things, they have been making dollar paper since 1879. The paper is produced in a special mill protected by federal guards. When the paper is shipped to Washington for engraving, it is as heavily guarded as the finished product. The recipe for dollar paper must fulfill difficult requirements. It must contain the proper proportion of colored threads and be strong enough to withstand four thousand double folds in the same spot without tearing.

Not far from Dalton, in Housatonic, Massachusetts, stands one of the grandest mills of the entire Berkshire region. The Rising Paper Company was

Above: Roslyn paper mill, Roslyn, Long Island, New York, 1773. Similar to a gristmill in construction, this mill used a waterwheel until 1882 when it was converted to steam. It ran until 1891. In 1790 George Washington visited the mill and tried his hand at papermaking. In 1915 it was restored by Harold Goodwin.

Photo Courtesy of Authors

The old stone mill of the Crane Paper Company in Dalton, Massachusetts, dates from 1844. It now houses the paper museum.

Photo Courtesy of Authors

Rising Paper Company mill, Housatonic, Massachusetts, c. 1873. Note the ornamental details, the heavy quoins and window lintels, the brickwork and the double-storied towers.

Photo Courtesy of Authors

started in 1873, the overly ambitious project of one Henry D. Cone, who, it seems, spent so much money building the ornate twin towers and adorning the two mill rectangles with heavy quoins and a mansard roof that he was not able to equip his mills. They were abandoned in 1878 as shells, with no machinery, and Mr. Cone went on to railroading. In 1899 B. D. Rising took them over and the Rising Paper Company has been making fine writing paper, wedding and announcement paper, and bristol and technical papers ever since. The buildings are quite impressive and large. The quoins and other ornamental trim are green, which is a pleasant diversion from the usual red brick and white trim of the cotton mills.

Although Maine and the northern parts of Vermont and New Hampshire are dotted with paper mills that make use of the pine forests of the North and Canada, we found only one worth recording. The bright yellow painted brick mill of the Pejepscot Paper Company in Topsham, Maine, dates from 1868. The waterwheels were located in a flume below the first floor now used for paper storage. The wooden addition is from 1874. The mill originally made rag papers, but soon switched to ground wood papers.

The building requirements of papermaking are much the same as those for textiles. Length rather than height is stressed, and there is the same need for uninterrupted interior space. It is difficult from the exterior to distinguish Rising or Pejepscot as paper companies, even though they are both rather individualistic in their use of ornament. It is safe to say that as textiles led the way in the industrial revolution, so textile factories set the pace for mill building in other industries.

Rising Paper Company mill, Housatonic, Massachusetts, c. 1873. Note the ornamental details, the heavy quoins and window lintels, the brickwork and the double-storied towers.   *Photo Courtesy of Authors*

The Hitchcock Chair Company, Riverton, Connecticut. The brick factory was built in 1826.

Photo Courtesy of Authors

THE ESTEY ORGAN CO.

IN BRATTLEBORO, VERMONT, THE NOW DEFUNCT ESTEY
Organ Company's complex of curious buildings still exists. They are remarkable
for one thing in particular. Slate was used to shingle the entire building, not just
the roof. What cannot be seen from a black-and-white photograph is the subtle
variety of colors the slate possesses. Shingles of this kind were probably costly
to apply because holes must be carefully drilled in each one before it can be
nailed down. The company had been plagued with so many fires, floods, and
mishaps that perhaps the owner wanted to use a less combustible material. Still,
slate is a curious choice. The series of buildings was begun around 1870. Brattleboro was something of a musical instrument center where violins, bass and double
bass viols, melodeons, seraphines, and Estey's reed organs and later pipe organs
were manufactured.

Jacob Estey knew nothing of music himself, having first been in business
making lead pipes and pumps for plumbing. He was a clever salesman and a
good administrator, however, and worked the company from a small shop to one
of the world's largest organ makers. In his factories many important innovations
and inventions were made by his skillful employees. When Estey bought into a
small melodeon shop in 1852, only six or seven instruments were made a year.
By 1902 the business had expanded to the production of large church pipe organs
and had sold 250,000 instruments.* The buildings are now either abandoned,
decaying, or used as bargain stores.

---

* *Annals of Brattleboro,* p. 634.

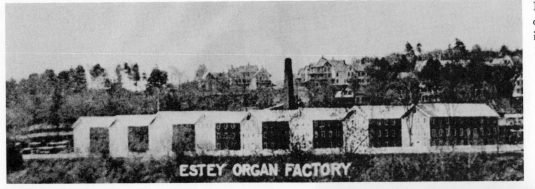

Eight slated factory buildings of the Estey Organ Company in Brattleboro, Vermont. After 1900.

Photo Courtesy Brooks Memorial Library, Brattleboro, Vermont

Above: Large pipe organ in Estey's erecting room, destined for a church in California.

Photo Courtesy Brooks Memorial Library, Brattleboro, Vermont

Rear of the factories of the Estey Organ Company as seen in 1970.

Photo Courtesy of Authors

THE HITCHCOCK CHAIR CO.

THE OLD HITCHCOCK CHAIR COMPANY IS SITUATED IN Riverton, formerly Hitchcocks-ville, in a still rural part of Connecticut. In the early 1800s Lambert Hitchcock from Cheshire, Connecticut, became interested in the new techniques of mass production that were being applied to the manufacture of wooden clock parts. After his apprenticeship to a cabinetmaker in Litchfield, he set up his first shop on the river near a sawmill. The brick factory, now painted white, was built in 1826 and was used at first to make only chair parts. It is probably more attractive now, even with subsequent additions, since the new Hitchcock Chair Company, which makes reproductions of the famous chairs and other furniture, has gone to some pain to refurbish the building, landscape the grounds, and create a showplace for their wares. Of course, the waterwheel and dam are no longer there and functioning. John T. Kenney and Richard E. Coombs must be credited with the idea of finding a profitable and extremely apropos use for a historic building.

Hitchcock's business was eventually quite successful. Under partnership the business expanded to the manufacture of larger cabinet pieces, including chests and mirrors. Items of high quality and enduring design were produced. Today they fetch astounding prices for dealers in Americana.

The Hitchcock Chair Company, Riverton, Connecticut, 1826, as it is today with its showroom and manufactory for Hitchcock reproductions. *Photo Courtesy of Authors*

THE AMERICAN OPTICAL CORP.

THE AMERICAN OPTICAL CORPORATION, NOW AN INTER-
national concern, had its humble beginnings above a jewelry shop in Southbridge,
Massachusetts. William Beecher, a farmer's son, developed tools and techniques
to make silver spectacle frames, which usually had to be imported from Europe.
This was around 1826. By 1843 he was making steel-rimmed spectacles, which
made a former luxury item affordable for most people who needed them. A
young employee, George Washington Wells, hired in 1868, proved to be such
an asset to the company with his mechanical genius that he ultimately gained
control of the company and ran it until 1952. The company expanded from
the manufacture of "spectacles of gold, silver, steel and plated metals, also rings
and thimbles"* in 1869 to countless other items, such as lenses, eye doctors'
diagnostic equipment, artificial eyes, and diverse medical and scientific instruments.

From the first little wooden store only thirty feet long with two floors and
a basement, the company grew into and then out of a series of handsome
mansard-roofed wooden buildings. The first of these was built in 1872. The
main part had four floors and a brick basement. As a safety precaution the walls
of the wooden structures were filled in with bricks and mortar. Additions in the

---

* "Historically Speaking . . . ," *The American Optical News*. Part 1, From the Beginning, vol. 2,
no. 7.

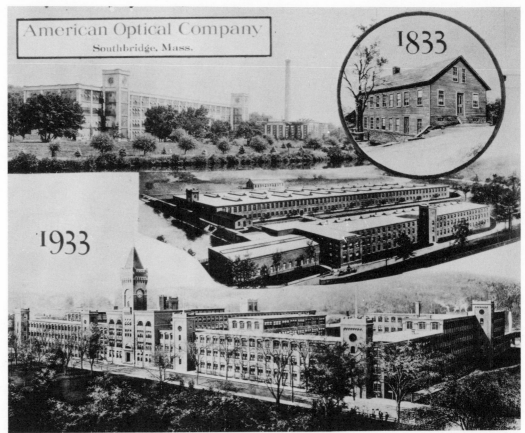

Centennial print of the American Optical Company, Southbridge, Massachusetts, showing little spectacle shop of 1833 and present mills.

Photo Courtesy
American Optical Company

The second group of factories of the American Optical Company dating from 1872. These buildings were on the site of the present brick factory.

Photo Courtesy
American Optical Company

Cloak room of the American
Optical Company in the early
1900s.

Photo Courtesy
American Optical Company

The lens pressing room of the
American Optical Company in
the late 1800s.

Photo Courtesy
American Optical Company

Frame manufacturing of the
American Optical Company
during the First World War.

Photo Courtesy
American Optical Company

The marble and wrought-iron staircase of the American Optical Company.

Photo Courtesy of Authors

same style were built, and the deep mansard roofs were flattened around the 1890s. Brick additions and reconstruction were started in 1899, and by 1902 the central tower building was complete. It is an imposing clock tower with crenellations and projecting water spouts that recall the gargoyles of cathedrals even though they are not figurative. The ornamental brickwork is polychrome and textured. The upper floor of this building has been called the banqueting hall.* There is a large formal room sixty-one by twenty-eight feet, a kitchen, library, and smaller serving room, none of which we could visit at the time of our trip to Southbridge. If the lobby was any indication of the rest, we were in awe that a factory building would have a marble staircase and elaborate banister fit for the White House.

The company also maintains a full staff of grounds keepers whose landscaping of the fifteen acres has won them awards. In the spring the American Optical Company's flower beds must be one of the pleasantest sights in Southbridge.

---

* "American Optical Company," read by George W. Wells at society meeting, November 29, 1906. *Quinabang Historical Society Leaflets*, vol. 2, no. 18, p. 184.

The elaborate clock-tower building is from 1902. The American Optical Company is very proud of its landscaping.

Photo Courtesy of Authors

4

PRESERVATION

PRESERVATION

NOW THAT WE HAVE SURVEYED THE EARLY INDUSTRIAL
architecture of the Northeast, it is time to give some thought to what can be done
to save and usefully preserve the best of it. The early mills, such as grist, saw,
and windmills, present different problems and require different solutions from
the large textile mills.

In the case of the small domestic mills, there are so few left that it is
reasonable to suggest that they should all be saved. Only by doing so will present
and future generations be able to directly experience the ways and uses of the
past. It would be a sorry thing indeed if only a book, such as this, were left to
tell their story. And yet, with very few exceptions, these mills are facing their
last days. Projects like Old Sturbridge Village and the Shelburne Museum are
fascinating and valuable collections and yet they are assemblages of buildings,
uprooted from the spots our ancestors carefully selected. To see structures in
their own environment is extremely important. There is no question of the right
of these old mills to exist; in no way do they hurt a natural, rural, or urban
environment. Instead, they teach respect for environment. What Stuart Udall,
former secretary of the interior, says about windmills may be applied to water
mills as well.

Windmills are much, much more than relics. They are symbols of
sanity for a world that is increasingly hooked on machines with an inordi-

Shaker Village gristmill, New Lebanon, New York, c. 1800. It was powered by a huge twenty-six-foot wheel.

Photo Courtesy of Authors

nate hunger for fuel and a prodigious capacity to pollute. . . . The issue is nobler than survival. It is whether we can equip ourselves to live truly decent lives. If we are to meet this challenge, our inventors and technicians will have to pay homage to windmills. They will have to build machines that use, not abuse, the unearned gifts of nature.*

Windmills have been more carefully respected than other domestic mills, perhaps because their forms are so remarkably picturesque and different from other architecture. Of the many that existed on Cape Cod, several have been restored and are open to the public. Some have survived by becoming part of residences, but this is a survival that entails compromises. They lose their vanes and sails; interiors must be severely modified to conform to modern standards of comfort, and they can no longer be explored and investigated by the public. There are, as well, the beautiful and authentic restorations in Rhode Island, Massachusetts, and New York.

Waterpowered gristmills have fared far worse. People have even seen fit to build copies, like the Ford mill near the Wayside Inn in Sudbury, Massachusetts, rather than restore old ones. And yet there is some hope that the

* *The New York Times*, February 13, 1971, p. 27.

◄

The remains of an overshot wheel at Stockbridge, Massachusetts.

Photo Courtesy of Authors

Probably a grist- and sawmill, Cooksburg, New York, c. 1840. This barn-red mill is in terrible condition. It resembles another mill in Cooksburg in that it too has a clerestory monitor. If repairs were made immediately, the gristmill could be saved.

Photo Courtesy of Authors

Windmill residence on the campus of Southampton College, Southampton, Long Island, New York, c. 1800. It is an example of a beautiful conversion.

Photo Courtesy of Authors

242

A former windmill on Cape Cod, now a residence. Although interesting as architecture, the windmill has lost its character by the removal of its sails and the insertion of large windows.

Photo Courtesy of Authors

Replica of an idealized gristmill. Built by Henry Ford, near the Wayside Inn, Sudbury, Massachusetts.

Photo Courtesy of Authors

undying romance of the waterwheel will save some mills, if only those people with the time and money could be diverted from tacking waterwheels to barn sides to work on the real thing. The remarkable thing about saving a gristmill is that it is very feasible to restore and refurbish it to perform its original task. More and more people, whom one is inclined to call wise rather than faddist, are demanding stone-ground flour. There is no reason why gristmills today cannot be profitably operated. At Weston, Vermont, the thriving Vermont Country Store has brought thousands of tourists to reexperience good old-fashioned atmosphere and articles. A nearby gristmill is currently being restored, this time as a tourist attraction and purveyor of wholesome grains. So profitable seems the enterprise that a second Vermont Country Store is now operating on Route 121 and a new waterpowered gristmill, made from old barn wood, is being erected on the same property. We have encountered few authentic grain mills that have continuously operated under waterpower. One such is a feed mill in Bernardston, Massachusetts, where animal feeds are ground. It is powered by a turbine and rope drive (see pp. 23, 50).

Another good use for a gristmill (impossible if it actually operates) is as a local history museum. In an out of the way town unused to or uninterested in tourist trade, a local museum or library operated by a historical society is a great asset for the inhabitants of the region. There also is no reason why a gristmill, if it could not be fully restored and operated, could not be maintained to absorb some social functions, such as dances and meetings, of the grange.

We have also seen gristmills that have been saved from oblivion by being used as restaurants (see pp. 18, 46). This necessitates additions for kitchens and seating space. In those we have seen it was not necessary to remove the stones, elevators, gears, or works, and a waterwheel has great drawing power. While such a use is not ideal and needs to be tastefully executed with a great amount of respect for the structure, it is a way to keep the building alive and paying its way.

Another use that does not entail adulteration of a mill's exterior is as an art gallery such as the seasonal one in Chester, Vermont. A mill can also be used as a local crafts center, as in Jericho, Vermont. These help to serve local communities and bring townspeople together.

To repeat, use as a residence entails major modification of a gristmill. Although it is an appealing notion to live in an old mill, it would be a greater service to find some other use.

Sawmills cause more of a problem when it comes to restoration. To begin with the structures were not always as carefully and solidly built as other mills. On occasion they were just thrown together to protect machinery. They are open on two or three sides so that any year-round use would necessitate great structural change or the large expense of installing Thermopane glass. The ideal usage, as with gristmills, would be the original one, but there is not the demand for up and down saw cuts that there is for stone-ground flour. In times when small and independent businesses are being squeezed out by large corporations,

Jewel mill, Rowley, Massachusetts, a reconstruction. It was built in 1643 on the site of the first fulling mill in America. Burned in 1965, it was rebuilt exactly as it was. An iron overshot wheel is used to power polishing tools for semiprecious stones.

Photo Courtesy of Authors

Decorative wheel on barnlike structure housing furniture samples at Hunt Country Furniture, Wingdale, New York.

Photo Courtesy of Authors

Above: New construction of a gristmill using old barn wood, Vermont Country Store, Route 121, near Cambridgeport, Vermont.
Photo Courtesy of Authors

Brookfield gristmill, Brookfield, Connecticut, 1780. Now an arts center.
Photo Courtesy of Authors

▶

Waterman's mill, Chester, Vermont, c. 1890. Was run by a turbine. It is now used as an art gallery.
Photo Courtesy of Authors

Old gristmill in Stockbridge, Massachusetts. Converted to a home.
Photo Courtesy of Authors

Burned shell of an old sawmill, Middleton, Massachusetts.
Photo Courtesy of Authors

it is less and less profitable for a small waterpowered mill to keep going. We know of only one that still uses a turbine to run a business, Masse's (see pp. 22, 56), in East Vassalboro, Maine. Atherton Bemis (see p. 54), whose mill is in Cavendish, Vermont, told us that he would still prefer the waterpower he gave up in 1940 if it weren't for the costs of repairs and maintenance that rose as people with old-time skills became rare.

There are, of course, valuable examples of waterpowered sawmills in museums, but they are few. In Greene, Rhode Island, Edwin Arnold, formerly connected with Old Sturbridge Village, made a little mill museum of his own. His property on a brook had been the site of successive grist and sawmills, as well as a blacksmith shop. Mr. Arnold acquired an up and down sawmill from Hopkinton, Massachusetts, and rebuilt it on his property to complement his gristmill of the 1840s. He also copied an old blacksmith shop from the same town, being careful to hire men who still knew the old way of building. A combination of preservation and knowledgeable reconstruction has brought to life a typical early industrial settlement.

There are so few sawmills left that it does not seem unreasonable to suggest that they should all be kept as sawmills to instruct and inform people of the present and the future. Such an impressive and complete structure as Mr. Woodruff's (see p. 67) could have many uses, since it is barnlike or even houselike. It is inhabited and loved by the Woodruff family, who have used it as a machine shop. They are rightly proud of their mill and have done little to alter or spoil it.

The early domestic mills were valuable and useful pieces of property in the past. Millsites in many instances saw a succession of mills over a period of many years. The mills themselves were subject to constant rebuilding and to modification of the power systems. Wooden wheels were replaced by metal ones and then turbines. It is not always easy to know to what state one should restore when a gristmill is being put back into service or simply put into a nonoperating state in which it is still possible to reexperience things as they were. Before deciding whether a waterwheel should be built, the age of the outstanding parts of the structure should be determined. It would be a shame to install a turbine in a mill where George Washington ate johnnycakes and where little else has happened since—would that there were many such mills! It would also be picturesque but inaccurate to put a wooden waterwheel on a mill from 1880 which was likely to have employed a turbine. The case is usually not so clear cut, and, along with age, cost must be considered.

Some types of mills are associated with a specific type of waterwheel. For example, the tub and flutter wheels were much used in early sawmills, and a good restoration should keep this in mind.

There is always the thin line that separates a restored mill from a totally reconstructed one. The Saugus ironworks has its attackers and defenders: those who believe all is based on solid archaeological and documentary evidence and those who believe it is largely the work of imagination. The truth is probably somewhere in between. The materials are almost entirely new, but the beautifully and faithfully crafted structures provide an accurate feeling for the period, and what is more, the entire complex functions, using its waterpower system. It is more than a surface rendering, for old methods of ironmaking can be dramatically demonstrated. In this way it is as authentic as a fine original gristmill grinding away by the power of a little electric motor disguised behind a purely decorative waterwheel.

With all the trouble and expense involved in the preservation of mills, authenticity should be the result.

Iron furnaces present a curious problem. They are extremely impressive as ruins, their arches of masonry recalling castles as much as anything. There are a few excellent examples of furnace-centered museums such as the Saugus works and the Sloane-Stanley Museum on the site of the Kent furnace in Kent, Connecticut. There a delightful small museum presents a display of early ironmaking, coupled with an exhibition of farm tools and implements, showing their uses. It gives a well-rounded picture of the inventiveness and ingenuity of the inhabitants of rural New England in a bygone era. It is a marvelously instructive glimpse at the past.

To restore the remaining iron furnaces to working order is neither desirable nor feasible. They are not suitable for habitation, restaurants, or community centers. However, the blast furnace was usually so solidly built that the tower-like structures are often sound or easily made so, and it seems much in a community's interest to see that they are maintained and kept in repair as a record of local industry and a model of old-time craftsmanship in masonry. The same can be said for charcoal kilns.

The larger industrial mills present a different set of problems and possible solutions. It is due to recent and present economic conditions that almost none of the old New England textile mills still turn out cloth. An impressive museum of the cotton industry has been set up in the old Slater mill in Pawtucket, Rhode Island, and wool has an artful display at the Merrimack Valley Textile Museum, which, however, is not housed in an old mill. One can use just so many such museums, so other mill uses must be found.

With textile mills it is not a question yet of restoring but of finding profitable, nondestructive uses for those that remain. A good many old mills, good and bad, have been torn down in decaying centers of industrial towns to make way for urban renewal. This has not always been wise policy. In Laconia, New Hampshire, it was only after a fierce fight that two beautiful mills, rare examples of brick mills from the 1820s (see p. 178), survived. And even after saving them, it looks as if imagination and a sense of design did not stretch far enough to integrate them into a meaningful plan with new structures that are going up around them.

Because textile mills are often located in the heart of towns, certain uses immediately suggest themselves. With the solid construction, high ceilings, and ample fenestration, a small- or medium-sized textile mill would make a fine department store without suffering too much alteration. Even sprinkler systems are to be found, ready to use in some cases. Of course, it is necessary that a town be of a size to support a department store, but how many suburban areas have been ruined by the hideous outgrowth of shopping plazas that could have been incorporated so tastefully in historic and useful existing structures. In the case of more cosmopolitan towns, a system of boutiques and arcades could be arranged in a textile mill to produce an effect like that of the Ghirardelli Square shops in San Francisco's mill-like old warehouses.

Another very constructive use of old mills is for housing. Typical mill placement beside a body of water is a great amenity, and the fact that mills are often in the center of towns might be considered an advantage for housing older people, small families, or those not interested in suburban life. By the same token a mill, reworked on the inside, could make an excellent school or nursing home. One factory owner, Moody C. Dole of Suncook, New Hampshire, went so far as to work up a proposal for his mill. China Mill Village was to be a retirement community on a forty-acre tract with over five thousand feet of river frontage. The 1868 brick mill is unusual in that it adjoins a town on one side but is completely spacious and open in the other direction. Mr. Dole proposed nature trails, gardening, boat docking, and, as the pollution controls for the Merrimack continue to operate, swimming and fishing facilities. It was heralded as breakthrough housing and historic preservation but was never funded.

Ruined mill at Potterville, Rhode Island.

Mills in process of destruction, North Adams, Massachusetts.

Busiel mill, Laconia, New Hampshire. This was taken while its fate was still uncertain and before later additions were stripped away. Condition: saved.

Photo Courtesy of Authors

China mill, Suncook, New Hampshire. This is the mill that at one time was proposed for a retirement community. Although not the most outstanding mill, its size and location near a town with lots of open space made such a project very feasible.

Photo Courtesy of Authors

Left: Artist's rendering of the south side of
the main building of the China mill; *Right:*
Aerial photograph at the junction of the
Suncook and Merrimack rivers.

From plans drawn for Moody C. Dole

Many are the small and larger mill towns with inadequate facilities for
old people and with beautiful empty mills awaiting demolition.

Another use for industrial buildings in the cosmopolitan cities is as housing
and studio space for artists. Again, the high ceilings, unpartitioned space, and
many windows are valuable assets. An experiment of this sort is underway in
Manhattan, where industrial buildings formerly used by Bell Laboratories now
house painters, dancers, musicians, designers, architects, photographers, and other
members of the artistic community who have enormous difficulty finding
adequate space for their work. Similarly, the smaller mills could be used by
YMCA–YMHA associations or youth hostels. They could also serve as adult
education and craft centers, as medical or office buildings, or even as town halls.

One interesting use for an entire community is being put into effect in
Quechee, Vermont. There a typical situation of a small mill community in a
rural setting is to be found. With the closing of the mills—Dewey Mills and the
Harris–Emery mill—the village rapidly lost population. Developers have come

An old mill and ruins are now a playhouse and falls overlook. This is a highly imaginative and beautiful use of an old woolen mill in Quechee, Vermont.

Photo Courtesy of Authors

into it, hoping to profit from the influx of tourists into beautiful Vermont. Theirs is not the typical one-or two-acre subdivision. They like to consider it a restoration and have been buying up antiques and old barns and farmhouses to keep their original outward appearance but to house new functions suited to twentieth-century tastes and activities. Certainly, with a large influx of second-homers, both the agricultural and early industrial character of the area will be lost, but what we have seen of the restoration is not cute or Yankeefied at all. They have chosen not to tear down the mill but have incorporated it into a cluster of tasteful new buildings and are going to use it for a playhouse. They have even left a row of brick window arches, part of the ruins of the mill, creating a strange space and interesting texture of materials. Over the stream, they have rebuilt a wooden-covered bridge carefully, authentically and with beautiful materials. One may object to vacation communities to begin with, but this, so far, is one of the most tasteful and imaginative we have seen. At least the developers are doing their best to preserve every old building, preserve its character, and preserve the open land.

The problems of large textile cities, what remains of them, are especially

◄

Westbeth, at West and Bethune streets, New York City. An old thirteen-story building formerly used by Bell Laboratories, it has been converted to artists' housing. Funded by the National Council on the Arts, the J. M. Kaplan Fund, and the FHA, and redesigned by Richard Meier to contain 383 apartment studios, it is a milestone in imaginative housing and preservation. Mr. Meier perhaps expresses its relevance best of all: "The aim is to make better quality of life without demolishing existing architecture."*   *Photo Courtesy David Gillison*

*"Westbeth" by Joel Baldwin, *Look* magazine, April 20, 1971.

great. Dependence upon a single industry proved disastrous when that industry failed, leaving population severely reduced and the center of town filled with enormous empty mills.

In these towns it was the total plan and organization, rather than individual mills, that merited study. But the problems of using so much mill space in financially depressed towns were too great. In Manchester a group of concerned people tried to avert total demolition by forming an association that rented mill space to a variety of separate industries and offices. Without enormous resources it is hard to imagine how to save an entire city. Yet it is hard to see why the beautiful boardinghouses of Lowell had to go or why those in Manchester should so seriously deteriorate when they could be pleasant places to live.

As for gigantic single mills, the late flowering of the Rhode Island pattern, especially in eastern Connecticut, it is difficult to suggest anything but another industry to take over from cotton. Depending on the industry, modification and modernization of the buildings would follow, but it is primarily the exterior of the later buildings that matters, and in that way they are more flexible than the old gristmill.

An entire town, such as Harrisville, New Hampshire, is unique.

The grant giving official recognition to the merits of early industrial architecture is an encouraging sign for the future.

APPENDIX

CANADA

MAINE

CANADA

NEW HAMPSHIRE

KENNEBEC R.

PENOBSCOT R.

ANDROSCOGGIN R.

● E.
Vassalboro

Lewiston

Portland

Biddeford

E. Lebanon

Kennebunkport

ATLANTIC
OCEAN

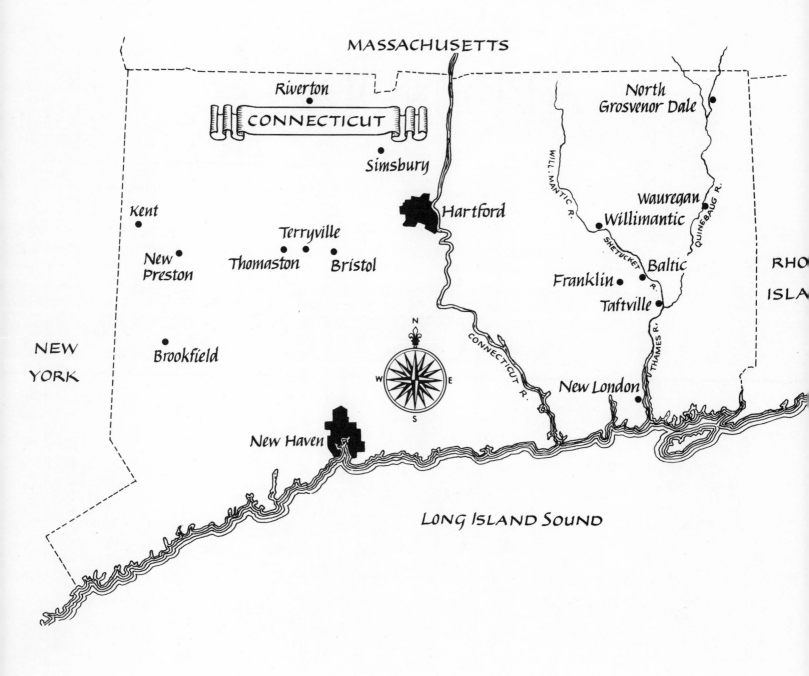

MASSACHUSETTS

Riverton

CONNECTICUT

Simsbury

North
Grosvenor Dale

Kent

Hartford

WILLIMANTIC R.

Wauregan
Willimantic

QUINEBAUG R.

Terryville

New
Preston

Thomaston

Bristol

SHETUCKET R.

Baltic

RHO
ISLA

Franklin

Taftville

NEW
YORK

Brookfield

N

W   E

S

CONNECTICUT R.

THAMES R.

New London

New Haven

LONG ISLAND SOUND

THE MILLS
AND WHERE THEY ARE

Use this list along with the maps to locate your favorite mill.

*The maps are arranged by state and include cities and towns.
The list is set up similarly, but also includes the names
of the mills and what city/town they are in.*

CONNECTICUT

Baltic cotton mill, Baltic
Brookfield gristmill, Brookfield
Eli Terry's waterwheel, Terryville
Franklin cider mill, Franklin
Gristmill, New London
Grosvenor Dale Company, North Grosvenor Dale
The Hitchcock Chair Company, Riverton
Iron furnace, Kent
Lewis Lock Company, Terryville
Ponemah mills, Taftville
Sawmill, New Milford
Seth Thomas, Thomaston
Wauregan mills, Wauregan
Willimantic Linen Company, Willimantic
Woodruff's sawmill, New Preston

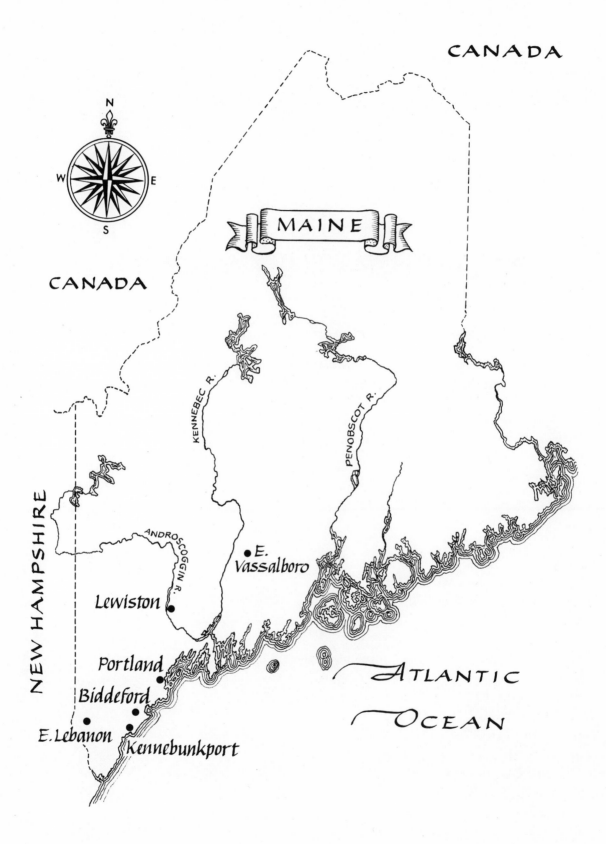

CANADA

N

W E

S

CANADA

MAINE

NEW HAMPSHIRE

KENNEBEC R.

PENOBSCOT R.

ANDROSCOGGIN R.

• E.
Vassalboro

Lewiston •

Portland •

Biddeford •

E. Lebanon •

Kennebunkport

ATLANTIC

OCEAN

MAINE

Continental mills, Lewiston
Little River mill, East Lebanon
Pepperell mills, Biddeford
Perkins tidewater gristmill, Kennebunkport
Sawmill and gristmill, East Vassalboro

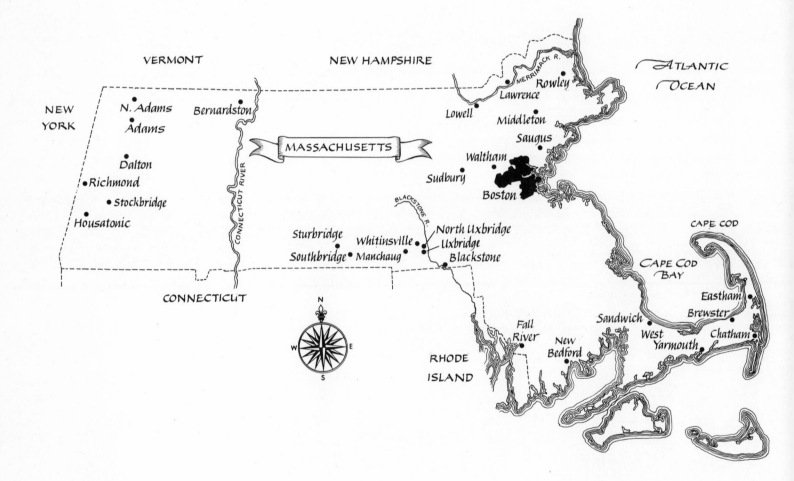

VERMONT   NEW HAMPSHIRE   ~ATLANTIC
~OCEAN

NEW
YORK

• N. Adams   Bernardston   MERRIMACK R.   • Rowley
  • Adams   Lawrence
                           Lowell •
  • Dalton   • Middleton
• Richmond   • Saugus
  • Stockbridge   MASSACHUSETTS   Waltham •
Housatonic   Sudbury •   Boston

                                                              CAPE COD

                                    BLACKSTONE R.   CAPE COD
                          Sturbridge •   Whitinsville • North Uxbridge   BAY
                          Southbridge • Manchaug   • Uxbridge   Eastham
                                                      Blackstone   Brewster
CONNECTICUT   Sandwich •   • Chatham
                                                                        West
                    N   Fall   Yarmouth
                  W   E   River   New
                    S   RHODE   Bedford
                                   ISLAND

264   APPENDIX

MASSACHUSETTS

American Optical Company, Southbridge
Baxter mill, West Yarmouth
B.B.R. Knight cotton mill, Manchaug
Carding mill, Old Sturbridge Village
Chaney up and down sawmill, Old Sturbridge Village
Chase mill, Fall River
Chatham gristmill, Chatham
Crane Paper Company, Dalton
Crown & Eagle, North Uxbridge
Eastham windmill, Eastham
First cotton mill, Fall River
Freeman Manufacturing Company, North Adams
Henry Ford gristmill, Sudbury
Iron furnace and countinghouse, Richmond
Ironworks, Saugus
Jewel mill, Rowley
J. L. Dunnell & Son feed mill, Bernardston
Linwood mill, Linwood
Mill, Maynard
Mills, Lawrence
Mills, tenements, and boardinghouses, Lowell
Monument mills, Housatonic
Northbridge cotton mill, Whitinsville
Old gristmill, Fall River
Old gristmill, Stockbridge
Old Machine Shop, Whitinsville
Pontoosuc woolen mill, Southbridge
The Rising Paper Company, Housatonic
Stony Brook gristmill, West Brewster
Talbot mill, North Billerica
Whitin Machine Works, Whitinsville
Wright gristmill, Old Sturbridge Village

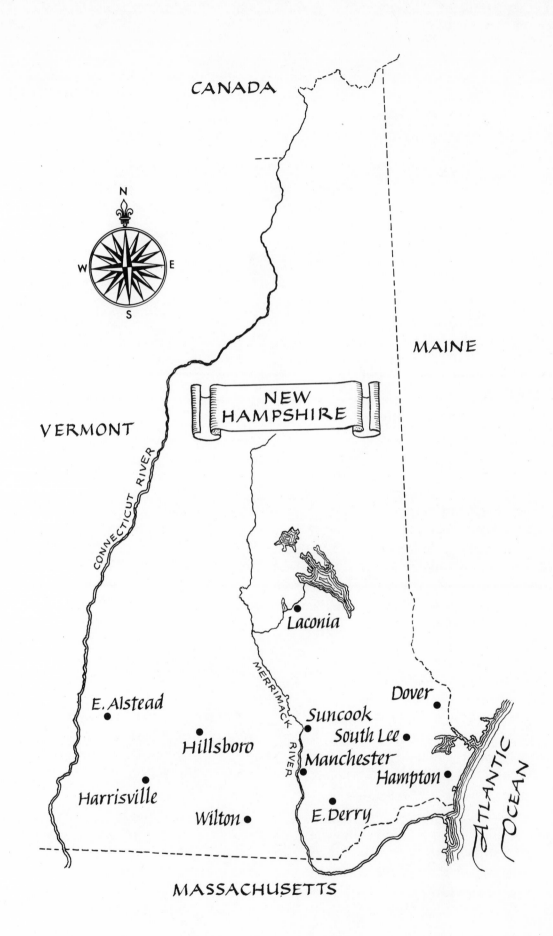

CANADA

MAINE

VERMONT

NEW
HAMPSHIRE

CONNECTICUT RIVER

Laconia

MERRIMACK RIVER

Dover

E. Alstead

Suncook

South Lee

Hillsboro

Manchester

Hampton

ATLANTIC OCEAN

Harrisville

Wilton

E. Derry

MASSACHUSETTS

APPENDIX

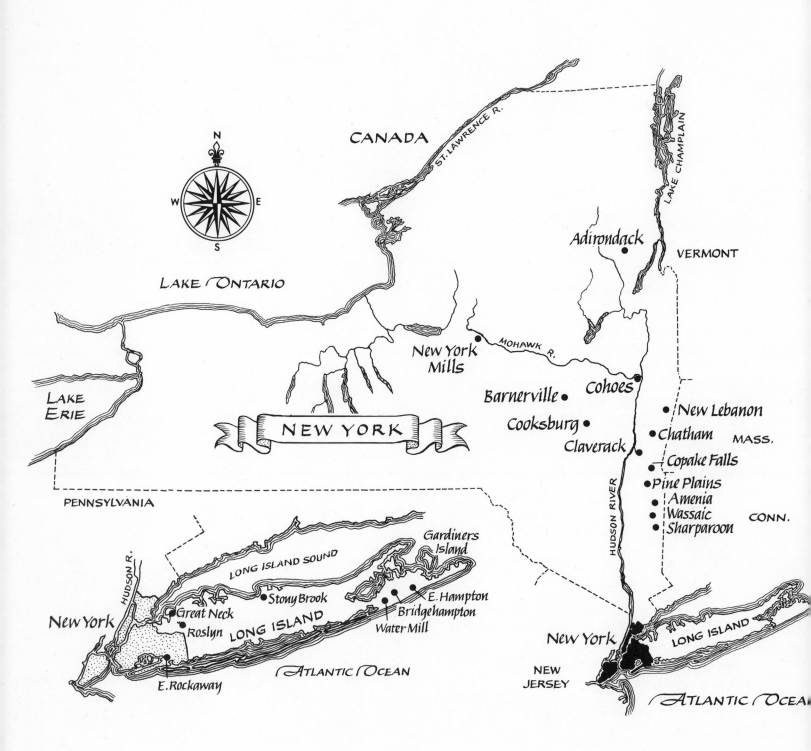

N
W E
S

CANADA

ST. LAWRENCE R.

LAKE CHAMPLAIN

Adirondack

VERMONT

LAKE ONTARIO

MOHAWK R.

New York Mills

Cohoes

Barnerville

Cooksburg

Claverack

New Lebanon

Chatham   MASS.

Copake Falls

Pine Plains

Amenia

Wassaic   CONN.

Sharparoon

LAKE ERIE

NEW YORK

HUDSON RIVER

PENNSYLVANIA

HUDSON R.

Gardiners Island

LONG ISLAND SOUND

Stony Brook

E. Hampton

Bridgehampton

Water Mill

New York

Great Neck

Roslyn

LONG ISLAND

Atlantic Ocean

E. Rockaway

New York

NEW JERSEY

LONG ISLAND

Atlantic Ocean

NEW YORK

Beebe gristmill, Bridgehampton, L.I.
Benkert's cider mill, Bethpage, L.I.
Carman's sawmill, Valley Stream, L.I.
Charcoal kilns, Wassaic
Cog mill, Port Washington
Davisons mill, East Rockaway, L.I.
Dover furnace, Sharparoon
East Marion mill, East Marion, L.I.
Gardiner mill, East Hampton, L.I.
Gerritsen tide mill, Brooklyn
Granite mill, New York Mills
Grist and sawmill, Cooksburg
Gristmill, Cold Spring Harbor
Harmony mills, Cohoes
Hicks mill, Westbury, L.I.
Hook mill, East Hampton, L.I.
Hunt Country Furniture, Wingdale
Iron furnace, Chatham
Iron furnace, Copake Falls
Isaac Satterly gristmill, Setauket, L.I.
MacIntyre furnace, Adirondack
Mill on Watts Pond, Valley Stream, L.I.
Pantigo mill, East Hampton, L.I.
Patchen grist and sawmills, Pine Plains
Plandome mill, Manhasset, L.I.
Red mill, Claverack
Roslyn gristmill, Roslyn, L.I.
Saddle Rock gristmill, Great Neck, L.I.
Shaker Village gristmill, New Lebanon
Thomas Chickering mill, Barnerville
Westbeth artists' housing, N.Y.C.
Windmill, Southampton, L.I.

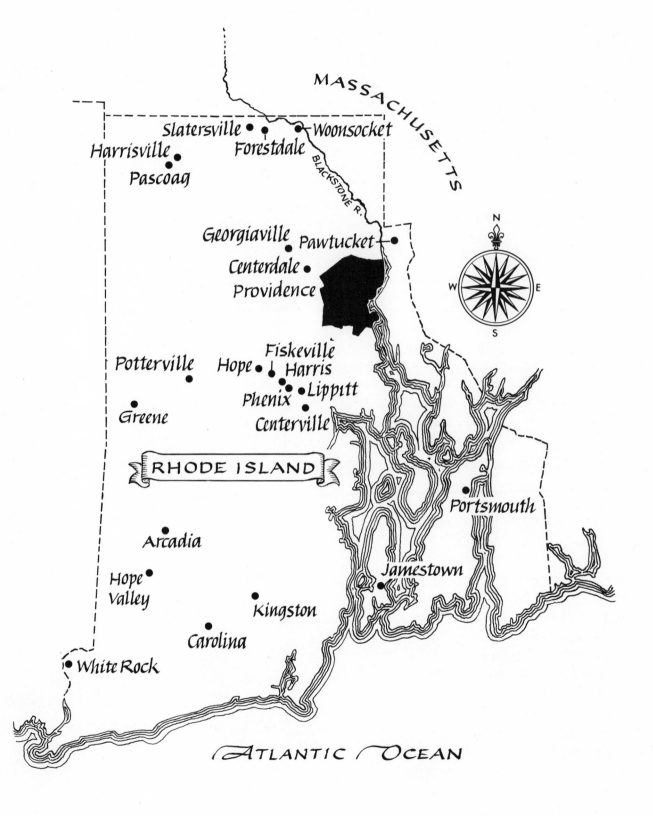

MASSACHUSETTS

Slatersville •
Forestdale •
• Woonsocket

Harrisville •

Pascoag •

BLACKSTONE R.

Georgiaville •
• Pawtucket

Centerdale •

Providence

N

W   E

S

Fiskeville
Potterville •
Hope •
Harris •

• Lippitt

Phenix •

Greene •
Centerville •

RHODE ISLAND

Portsmouth •

Arcadia •

Hope •
Valley

Jamestown •

Kingston •

Carolina •

• White Rock

ATLANTIC OCEAN

RHODE ISLAND

A. L. Sayles mill, Pascoag
Allendale mill, North Providence
Butterfly mill, Lincoln
Clinton mill, Woonsocket
Cotton mill, Carolina
Cotton mill, Centerville
Cotton mill, Davisville
Cotton mill, Quidnick
Cotton mill village, Hope
Fiskeville cottages, Fiskeville
Georgiaville cottages, Georgiaville
Governor Harris mill, Harris
Gristmill, North Kingston
Hampton mill village, Hampton
Harris mill village, Harris
Jamestown gristmill, Jamestown
Lippitt mill, Lippitt
Lippitt woolen mill, Woonsocket
Merino mill, Providence
Old Slater Mill Museum, Pawtucket
Phenix mill village, Phenix
Portsmouth gristmill, Portsmouth
Ruined mill, Potterville
Sheffield worsted mill, Pascoag
Slatersville mill village, Slatersville
Snuff mill, North Kingston
Stamina mill, Forestdale
Up and down sawmill, Greene
White Rock mill, White Rock

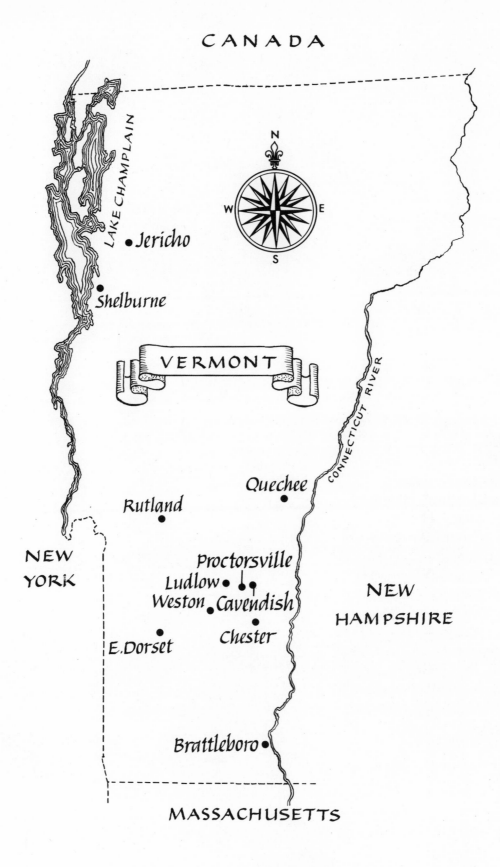

CANADA

LAKE CHAMPLAIN

• Jericho

• Shelburne

VERMONT

CONNECTICUT RIVER

• Quechee

Rutland •

Proctorsville
Ludlow • •
Weston • Cavendish
• Chester

NEW
YORK

• E.Dorset

NEW
HAMPSHIRE

Brattleboro •

MASSACHUSETTS

VERMONT

Atherton Bemis grist and sawmill, Cavendish
Blow Me Downe mill, Plainfield
Dewey mills, Quechee
Estey Organ Company, Brattleboro
Gaymont Woolen Company, Ludlow
Iron furnace, East Dorset
Jericho mill, Jericho
New gristmill of Vermont Country Store near Cambridgeport
Old Murdock mill, Proctorsville
Sawmill, Irasburg
Up and down sawmill, Shelburne Museum, Shelburne
Up and down sawmill, Vermont Guild Museum, Weston
Waterman's mill, Chester

GLOSSARY

BED STONE. *See* Nether stone.

BILL. *See* Millstone picker.

BLAST FURNACE. The structure wherein ore is reduced to metal. *Blast* refers to the stream of air consistently introduced to maintain the fire within the furnace.

BOLTING. The sifting of flour into various grades of fineness.

BRAKE WHEEL. A large wheel within a windmill attached to the wind shaft in the fashion of a face wheel. On it a wooden band or strap was tightened to stop the rotation of the sail arms.

BREAST WHEEL. A vertical wheel rotated by the weight and percussion of water striking a series of buckets slightly above or below the wheel's axle. If it struck above, it was called a high breast wheel, and if it struck below, a low breast wheel.

BUCKETS. A series of enclosed paddles struck by water utilizing its force and weight to power both breast and overshot wheels.

CARDING. The process whereby the fibers of wool or cotton are combed, straightened, and aligned before they undergo spinning into yarn.

CHAFFERY HEARTH. An open furnace or forge where iron is reheated to be wrought into bars.

CHARGE. The mixture of ore, charcoal, and flux, which is heated in the furnace to refine iron ore.

CHARGE HOLE. The opening in the top of the furnace down which the charge is put for heating.

CLERESTORY MONITOR. An attic lighting device comparable to the trap-door monitor but extending the length of the roof to the edge of the building.

CORBELING. A supporting or decorative projection from the face of a wall. In Romanesque factory architecture corbeling usually consisted of a series of small arches along a cornice usually worked in brick.

CORN SHELLER. A hand-cranked machine that consisted of two pieces of rotating boards studded with many iron points or nails. When an ear of corn was placed between them, the rotating nailheads shelled the corn.

CORNICE. The top part of a wall when accented or ornamented in such a fashion as to distinguish it.

> BRACKETED CORNICE. A cornice whose ornamental features consist of brackets of more or less complex design and whose function is more ornamental than supportive.

CRENELLATIONS. Battlements typical of castle architecture.

CRUCIBLE. A pot, sometimes of clay or porcelain, or a hollow at the bottom of a furnace where melted metal is received.

DAMSEL. A small forked instrument attached to the rind projecting through the eye of the runner. It lightly tapped the shoe, causing grain to drop into the eye of the runner.

DECKLE. An irregular edge of a piece of paper that formed the overflow of pulp on the mold.

DORMER. Vertical windows in a sloping roof.

DRAFT TUBE. A tube having one end attached to the turbine and its other submerged in the tailrace. It channeled and pressurized the water used by the turbine into the tailrace.

EYE. The hole in the runner stone.

FACE WHEEL. A gear wheel attached to the waterwheel shaft.

FALL. The action of water on a wheel below the point of impact, the gravity stage. *See also* Head.

FANTAIL. Small windwheel placed opposite the sail arms on the cap of a windmill. Its function was to keep the cap adjusted to the wind.

FEED POLE. A rod that was connected to the rack wheel that, when adjusted, determined the rate of advance of the log toward the saw.

FENDER POSTS. Greased side blocks that guided and steadied the motion of the saw frame.

FINERY HEARTH. The open hearth where pig iron was heated and further refined. An intermediate stage coming before final heating in the chaffery hearth and fashioning into merchant bars.

FINEST. Designation of the best flour.

FLOAT WHEEL. Basically an undershot wheel either mounted between two anchored pontoons or boats or in pairs on either side of a single anchored boat or pontoon. It was powered by the swiftness of the river's current and therefore needed no dam.

FLUME. *See* Sluiceway.

FLUTTER WHEEL. Basically an undershot wheel with a series of long paddles connected to arms radiating from a shaft. The name flutter was given to this wheel because of the birdlike sound it makes when its paddles cut through the water.

FLUX. The material which when heated with ore fuses with and removes the impurities, thereby refining the ore to metal.

FLYER. *See* Fantail.

FRENCH BUHRSTONE. The most sought after stone for millstones. It was quarried in the Paris basin.

FULLING. The process whereby woolen cloth is cleaned, shrunken, and felted to give it the desired texture and consistency.

FURROWS. A pattern of cuts on the bottom of the runner and top of the nether stones. Furrows sheared the grain's outer husk and channeled the grain along, delivering it to the "land" and ultimately to the outer edge of the stones. They also vented the stones, removing some of the heat created by friction during the grinding process.

GABLE (ROOF). A gable is a vertical triangular portion of the end of a building, from the cornice or eaves to the ridge of the roof. A gabled roof is a roof forming a gable at each end.

GAMBREL ROOF. A roof having a double slope.

GRAPPLING HOOKS. A pair of hooks attached to a screw hoist or small crane used for raising the runner stone.

"GREEK MILL." *See* Norse mill.

GRIST. Grain ground in the mill, originally corn, later applied to all grains.

GRISTMILL.   A place where grain was ground into meal and/or flour. *See* Grist.

GUDGEONS.   Iron sleeves that fit over a section of the horizontal shaft and side of a vertical waterwheel.

GUIDE BLADES.   A series of blades arranged around the runner and curved in the opposite direction that channeled water to the runner.

HEAD.   The distance water falls to the point of impact against a wheel, the percussion stage.

HIGH BREAST WHEEL.   *See* Breast wheel.

HINGED COGS.   Iron clamps that could be adjusted to determine how thick a log would be sawed.

HIP ROOF.   A roof having sloping ends and sloping sides.

HOLLANDER.   A machine used to macerate rags.

HOOP.   *See* Vat.

HOPPER.   A four-sided tapering wooden chute placed above and to the side of the eye of the runner.

HOPPER BOY.   A revolving rake and spreader used to dry and cool flour.

HORIZONTAL MILL.   *See* Norse mill.

HORIZONTAL WHEEL.   A shaft holding a rotor at one end.

LAND.   An area on the millstone left uncut between the furrows, which functioned as a grinding surface.

LANTERN GEAR.   A gear resembling a lantern containing a series of vertical dowels mortised between two horizontal wooden disks used to transform horizontal gearing to vertical and vice-versa.

LOW BREAST WHEEL.   *See* Breast wheel.

MACE-HEAD.   A bracket mounted at the top of the spindle to which was attached the rind.

MANSARD ROOF.   Named after its inventor. A curved roof line, often sloping back in a convex fashion.

MERCHANT BARS.   Large bars of wrought iron that blacksmiths obtained from furnaces and from which they fashioned their wares.

MIDDLINGS.   Designation of mediocre flour.

MILL FLEAM.   *See* Sluiceway.

MILL PICK.   *See* Millstone picker.

MILL RUN.   *See* Sluiceway.

MILL WASH.   *See* Milltail.

MILL WAY.   *See* Sluiceway.

MILLRACE.   A ditch, trough, or pipe made of earth, wood, iron, or cement that conveyed the water from the dam to the sluiceway.

MILLSTONE PICKER.   The man who cut, repaired or sharpened the furrows, in the millstone. His tool was the mill pick, or bill. Bills were first made of iron, which tended to dull and chip easily. The tip was eventually replaced by steel.

MILLTAIL.   The water remaining after it had turned the wheel or turbine.

MOLD.   A wooden frame for papermaking with a close wire mesh that was dipped into the pulp.

MORTISE-JOINT CONSTRUCTION.   The cutting of a slot in one member and forming a corresponding tenon or tongue in another. The two were held together by a treenail or wooden peg inserted in a hole drilled through both members.

NAP.   The woolly or brushed surface of a fabric usually created by some sort of abrasion.

NETHER STONE.   The bottom millstone.

NORSE MILL.   The earliest type of water mill, often called the Greek or horizontal mill. It consisted of a shaft that at one end had a rotor that was propelled by the force of a moving stream and at the other the runner stone.

OVERSHOT.   *See* Overshot wheel.

OVERSHOT WHEEL.   A vertical wheel where the weight and percussion of water strikes a series of buckets on the outer circumference of the wheel.

PEDIMENT.   From classical architecture. The triangular space forming the gable of a roof.

PENSTOCK.   The same as a millrace but in reference to the turbine; it is the final chute that delivers water to the machine.

PIG IRON.   The iron run directly from the furnace after melting. Usually it is cast into molds or bars called "pigs."

PILASTER.   An ornamented device resembling a column not freely disengaged and supportive but flat to a wall or facade acting as a pier.

PITCH-BACK WHEEL.   Similar to an overshot wheel except the water hit the wheel at its top edge causing it to revolve in a counterclockwise direction (toward instead of away from the sluiceway).

PITMAN.   The man who worked in a sawpit pulling down on the saw.

PITMAN ROD.   A long rod that attached the saw frame to a crank.

PLANING MILL.   A mill that was capable of producing smooth boards.

PLUMPING MILL.   A primitive water mill where a pounder was raised by the weight of water filling a bucket at one end. When the bucket descended, the pounding head was raised; as the water spilled out, the pounder descended by its own weight.

POST.   The formed sheet removed from the mold.

POST-MILL.   A type of windmill whose works were encased in a structure raised on a post and rotated thereon to face the winds.

RACE.   *See* Millrace.

RACK WHEEL.   A wheel that inched the carriage holding the log toward the saw.

ROLLING AND SLITTING MILL.   A mill where heated and softened metal is rolled in sheets and slit or cut into strips to make nails, barrel hoops, and the like.

ROPE DRIVE.   A system of ropes or more commonly leather straps used to transmit power from its source, such as a turbine or generator, either horizontally or vertically.

ROTARY QUERN MILL.   The same as a stone quern mill except that the stones were set in a boxlike structure with a hole through which the runner stone handle projected.

ROVING.   When cotton or wool are carded, the result, a long soft preliminary yarn, is called the roving. It consists of the straightened and aligned fibers before they have been twisted into the final yarn.

RUNNER.   A vertical shaft having a series of blades emanating from its center.

RUNNER STONE.   The top and/or revolving millstone.

RYND.   An iron bar attached to the mace-head that fitted into the two or four out cuts holding the runner stone.

SAIL BARS.   The crosswise markers of the gridlike wooden structure of the sail arms of a windmill.

SAPLING AND STUMP MILL.   A mill where a pounding tool was attached to a sapling in order to use its spring action. A hollow tree trunk housed the grain to be pounded.

SAWYERS.   Men who sawed logs.

SHOE. A narrow wooden trough that hung loosely over the eye that when gently tapped fed grain in a slow and steady way, preventing the clogging of the eye of the runner.

SHORTS. Designation for the most undesirable flour.

SIZING. The process that produces the desired surface on a sheet of paper.

SLAG. The impurities refined out of metal.

SLUICE GATE. A gate that opened and closed, regulating the amount of water reaching the wheel or turbine from the sluiceway.

SLUICEWAY. The final passage through which the water flowed before reaching the wheel.

SMOCK MILL. A windmill with a revolving cap resembling a smock.

SPILLWAY. *See* Milltail.

SPINDLE. The vertical shaft upon which rested the runner stone.

STEP BEARING. A screwlike device used to adjust the distance between two millstones by raising or lowering the runner stone.

STOCK. A tapering shaft (the major structural member of the sail) mortised or wedged at its widest end to the wind shaft.

STONE QUERN. This consisted of a stationary stone and the top or runner stone, which was rotated by hand.

TAIL. *See* Milltail.

TAILPIECE. A long pole used to turn the cap of a smock mill and the entire mill structure of a post-mill into the wind.

TAILRACE. *See* Milltail.

TEASEL. A prickly plant that, when dried, was used to raise a nap on woolen cloth or to card wool fibers.

TENEMENT. In a discussion of mill housing, this does not refer to a slum dwelling but to a rented or "tenanted" house.

TIDE WHEEL. A type of undershot wheel powered by the tidal flow.

TOLL. Payment in the form of a percentage given to the miller for work done on grain ground.

TOP SAWYER. The man who pulled up on the saw and guided it along.

TRAP-DOOR MONITOR. Also called "eyebrow" monitor. An attic lighting device that looks as if a section of roof has been raised, like a trap door in a floor.

TUB WHEEL.   A horizontal wheel midway between a Greek mill and turbine. The horizontal wheel was mounted in a tub constructed of wooden slats and reinforced with iron hoops. It received water via a sluiceway in the form of a tube that entered the tub at an angle. The water rotated the wheel by percussion.

TURBINE.   A modified tub wheel with greater power and efficiency. It consisted of a system that fed water to the runner through guide blades arranged around the rim of the runner and curved in the opposite direction from the runner's vanes. In this way water flowed through the machine in the opposite direction from the water in the tub wheel and created a great force.

TURNING MILL.   A mill capable of producing round wooden members.

TUYERE.   A pyre through which passed a stream of air from the bellows to the furnace.

UNDERSHOT WHEEL.   A vertical wheel rotated by the percussion of water striking a series of paddles at the base of the wheel.

UPLONGS.   The lengthwise members of the gridlike wood structure of the sail arms of a windmill.

VAT.   A wooden box in which the stones were enclosed.

WALLOWER.   *See* Lantern gear.

WASTEWAY.   *See* Milltail.

WATERMARK.   A design embedded into the paper formed by a pattern woven into the wire mesh of the mold.

WHIPS.   *See* Uplongs.

WIND SHAFT.   The shaft that held the sail assembly at one end and was geared to the remaining machinery at the other.

SELECTED BIBLIOGRAPHY

Abbott, Edith. *Women in Industry.* New York: D. Appleton & Co., 1910.

Armstrong, John Borden. *Factory Under the Elms: A History of Harrisville, New Hampshire, 1774–1969.* Cambridge, Massachusetts: M.I.T. Press for Merrimack Valley Textile Museum, 1969.

Bagnall, William R. *The Textile Industries of the United States.* Vol. I. Cambridge, Massachusetts, 1893.

Browne, George Waldo. *The Amoskeag Manufacturing Company of Manchester, New Hampshire: A History.* Printed and bound in the mills of Amoskeag, 1915.

Chase, Herman. *Short History of Mill Hollow.* Springfield, Vermont: Edmund and Mary Hurd, 1964.

Clarke, Mary Stetson. *Pioneer Iron Works.* Philadelphia: Chilton Book Company, 1968.

Cole, Arthur Harrison. *The American Wool Manufacture.* 2 vols. Cambridge, Massachusetts: Harvard University Press, 1926.

Cole, Jessie S. "The Song of the Damsel." *Yankee,* May 1970.

Coleman, Richard. "The Oldest Mill, to Be or Not to Be." *Yankee,* June 1971.

Coolidge, John. *Mill and Mansion: A Study of Architecture and Society in Lowell, Massachusetts, 1820–1865.* New York: Russell and Russell, 1967.

Copeland, Melvin Thomas. *The Cotton Manufacturing Industry of the United States*. New York: Augustus M. Kelley, 1966.

Craik, David. *Practical Millwright and Miller*. Philadelphia: Henry Carey Baird & Co., 1882.

Evans, Oliver. *The Young Millwright and Millers Guide*. Philadelphia, 1795.

Fairbairn, William. *Treatise on Mills and Millwork*. London: Green, Longman, Roberts and Green, Inc., 1864.

Fennelly, Catherine. *Textiles in New England, 1790–1840*. Sturbridge, Massachusetts: 1961.

Freese, Stanley. *Windmills and Millwrighting*. New York: Cambridge University Press, 1957.

Gallivan, John. "The Great Wheels Turning." *Yankee*, August 1963.

Grieve, Robert. *The Cotton Centennial 1790–1890*. Providence, Rhode Island: J. A. & R. A. Reid, 1891.

Hamilton, Edward P. *The Village Mill in Early New England*. Sturbridge, Massachusetts: Old Sturbridge Village Booklet Series, 1964.

Historic American Buildings Survey, some textile mill inventory notes, unpublished survey. Connecticut Historical Commission, Hartford.

Hitchcock, Henry Russell. *Rhode Island Architecture*. Cambridge, Massachusetts: M.I.T. Press, 1968.

Huxtable, Ada Louise. "New England Mill Village, Harrisville, New Hampshire." *Progressive Architecture in America*, vol. 38, pp. 139–40, July 1957.

James Leffel and Co., 1870–1920, descriptive pamphlets, Springfield, Ohio.

Jaray, Cornell. *The Mills of Long Island*. Port Washington, New York: Ira J. Friedman, Inc., 1962.

Josephson, Hannah. *The Golden Threads: New England's Mill Girls and Magnates*. New York: Russell and Russell, 1967.

"Lambert Hitchcock of Hitchcocks-ville, Connecticut: America's Most Famous Chairmaker and the Story of His Original Manufactory." *Bulletin*, The Antiquarian and Landmarks Society Inc. of Connecticut, vol. XVIII, no. 1, July 1966.

Langenbach, Randolph. "Amoskeag: An Epic in Urban Design." *Industrial Archaeology*, 1968.

———. "The Amoskeag Case: Must We Destroy Our Past to Renew Our Cities?" *Harvard Alumni News*, vol. 70, no. 12, April 13, 1968.

Lincoln, Jonathan T. "The Beginning of the Machine Age in New England: David Wilkinson of Pawtucket." *New England Quarterly*, vol. VI, 1933.

Marshall, Bernice. *The Water Mills of Long Island*. Port Washington, New York: Ira J. Friedman, Inc., 1962.

Martin, Donald W. "East Vassalboro's Old Watermill Still Going Strong." *Down East*, vol. XVIII, No. 4, November 1971.

———. "To Find a Mill." *Yankee*, April 1971.

Masters, Arthur H. *The History of Cohoes, New York, From Its Earliest Settlement to the Present Time*. Albany: J. Munsell, 1877.

Merrimack Valley Textile Museum, Wool Technology and the Industrial Revolution: An Exhibit. North Andover, Massachusetts, 1971.

Navin, Thomas R. *The Whitin Machine Works Since 1839: A Textile Company in an Industrial Village*. Cambridge, Massachusetts: Harvard University Press, 1950.

Orton, Ellen and Vrest. *Cooking with Whole Grains*. New York: Farrar, Straus and Giroux, Inc., 1951.

Palmer, Brooks. *The Romance of Time*. New Haven: Clock Manufacturers Association of America, Inc., date unknown.

Pierson, William. "The Industrial Architecture of the Berkshires." Doctoral dissertation presented at Yale University, May 1949.

Rawson, Marion Nicholl. *Little Old Mills*. New York: E. P. Dutton and Co., Inc., 1935.

Reynolds, John. *Windmills and Watermills*. New York: Praeger Publishers, Inc., 1970.

Rhode Island Mills and Mill Villages. Photographs made for the Nickerson Architectural Collection, Providence, Rhode Island, Public Library by Joseph McCarthy under the auspices of the Federal Works Agency of the Works Progress Administration, 1940. Text, catalogue of photographs, chronological outline by Samuel Green. Unpublished.

Rich, Les. "Quechee: A Vermont Dilemma." *Yankee*, April 1971.

Sangster, John R. *Seth Thomas: A Yankee Clockmaker*, date unknown.

The Saugus Iron Works Restoration. Saugus, Massachusetts: First Iron Works Association, 1951.

Shea, John G. *The American Shakers and Their Furniture*. New York: Van Nostrand Reinhold, 1971.

Shelton, F. H. "Windmills, Picturesque and Historic: The Motors of the Past." *Journal of the Franklin Institute*, 1919.

Sloane, Eric. *Our Vanishing Landscape*. New York: Funk and Wagnalls, 1955.

Smith, Page. *As a City Upon a Hill: The Town in American History*. New York: Alfred A. Knopf, 1966.

Stokhuyzen, Frederick. *The Dutch Windmill*. New York: Universe Books, Inc., 1963.

"Town for Sale." *Yankee,* March 1971.

Wailes, Rex. *Windmills of Eastern Long Island*. Port Washington, New York: Ira J. Friedman, Inc., 1962.

Ware, Caroline F. *Early New England Cotton Manufacture: A Study in Industrial Beginnings.* New York: Russell and Russell, 1966.

Weiss, Harry B., and Ziegler, Grace M. "The Early Fulling Mills of New Jersey." *New Jersey Agricultural Society of Trenton,* 1957.

Wells, George G. "The American Optical Company." *Quinabaug Historical Society Leaflets,* vol. 2, no. 18, date unknown.

"The White Rock Mill." *The Narragansett Weekly,* August 23, 1877.

Wymelenberg, Suzanne Van Den. "Amoskeag: The Last Chance of the Great New England Mills." *Yankee,* October 1968.

INDEX

Runner stone, 11, *14*, 25, *30*, 31, 32, *78*, 280
Rutland, Vt., *272*

S

Saco, Maine, 169
Saddle Rock gristmill (Great Neck, N.Y.), *17*, *33*, *36*, 269
Sag Harbor, N.Y., *80*
Sails, 70, 72, 76, 80, *82*, 83
Sandwich, Mass., *264*
Sapling and stump mill, *26*, 280
Satterly gristmill (Setauket, N.Y.), *49*, 269
Saugus, Mass., *264*
  ironworks, 83–84, *84*, 85, *85*, *94*, 95, *95*, *96*, 250, 265
Sawmills, 22, 37, 51, *52*, *54*, *55*, *56*, *57*, 58, *59*, *60*, *61*, *62*, *63*, 64, *65*, *66*, *67*, *68*, 83, 98, 239, 244, 249, *249*, 250, 261, 263, 265, 267, 269, 271, 273
Sawyer woolen mills (Dover, N.H.), *157*, 267
Sawyers, 51, 58, 280
Sayles mill (Pascoag, R.I.), *122*, 136, *138*, *140*, 271
Schofield, Arthur, 103, 205
Schofield, John, 103, 205
Scituate, Mass., 58
Setauket, N.Y., *49*, *268*
Shakers, 58, 107, *241*, 269
Sharparoon, N.Y., *92*, *268*
Sheffield worsted mill (Pascoag, R.I.), *122*, 271
Shelburne, Vt., *272*
Shelburne Museum (Vt.), 239
Shingle-clapboard mill (East Lebanon, Maine), *53*
Shorts, 38, 281
Shovel, wooden, *36*
Silvermine, Conn., 58
Simsbury, Conn., *51*
Slater, Samuel, 108, 109, *110*, 110–12, *123*, 141, 149, 150, 166, 207
Slater mill (Pawtucket, R.I.), *110*, 112, 251
Slatersville, R.I., *123*, 150, *152*, *164*, *270*
Slitting mills, *84*, 95, *96*, 280
Sloane-Stanley Museum (Kent, Conn.), 250
Slubbing Billy, 207
Sluiceway, 7, 9, 16, *20*, 21, 65, *65*, 99, 281
Smith, John Butler, *213*

Smock windmills, 72, *73*, 76, 281
Snuff mills, *43*, 97, *97*, 98, *98*, 281
South Lee, N.H., *55*, *57*, *266*
South Royalton, Vt., *59*
South Waterford, Maine, *20*, 104, *104*
Southampton, N.Y., *242*, *268*
Southbridge, Mass., 206, 207, 231, *232*, 234, *264*
Spindle, 32, 281
Spinning frame, 111
Spinning jenny, 108
Spinning mills, 112
Sprague, Conn., 141
Stamina mill (Forestdale, R.I.), *122*, 271
Stark Mills (Manchester, N.H.), *179*
Steam power, 108, 187, 188, 192
Steel, *93*, 94
Stevens mill (North Andover, Mass.), *188*
Stockbridge, Mass., 224, *241*, *248*, *264*
Stone quern, 25, 27, 281
Stony Brook, N.Y., *43*, *268*
Stony Brook gristmill (Stony Brook, N.Y.), *43*
Stores, mill, *155*, 164
Stratford, Conn., 28
Strutt, Jedediah, 109
Stuart, Gilbert, *43*, 97, 98
Sturbridge, Mass., *264*. *See also* Old Sturbridge Village
Sudbury, Mass., 241, *243*, *264*
Suncook, N.H., 251, *254*, *266*
Swedish mill (Cobb's Creek, Philadelphia), *10*

T

Taftville, Conn., 136, *140*, 153, *155*, 165, *260*
Talbot mill (North Billerica, Mass.), *135*, 265
Taunton, Mass., 169
Taylor sawmill (East Derry, N.H.), *63*, 267
Terry, Eli, 217, *218*, 219, 261
Terry, James, 217, *219*
Terryville, Conn., 217, *218*, *219*, *260*
Textile mills, 105–213, 239, 251
Thomas, Seth, 217, 219, 220, *220*, *221*, *222*, 261
Thomaston, Conn., 219, *260*
Tide mills, 7, *9*, 16, *17*, *18*, 28
Tide wheels, 16, 281
Topsham, Maine, 226

Towns, mill. *See* Villages, mill
Trap-door monitor, 112–13, *118*, 150, 281
Treadmill, 25
Trescott, Jeremiah, *59*
Tub wheels, 19–21, 64, *65*, 250, 281
Tullers gristmill (Simsbury, Conn.), *51*
Turbines, 21, *21*, 22, *22*, *23*, *24*, 95, 99, 112, 130, 187, 200, 244, 249, 250, 282

U

Udall, Stuart, 239
Undershot wheels, 15, *15*, 282
Upton, Mr., *138*
Utica, N.Y., 200
Utica Cutlery Company, 200
Uxbridge, Mass., *264*

V

Valley Stream, N.Y., *43*, *66*, *268*
Van Rensselaer, Jacob R., 47
Van Rensselaer, Stephen, 197
Vat, 32, 282
Vertical wheels, 11, 36
Villages, mill, 150, *151*, *152*, 153, *153*, *154*, 156, *157*, 158, *161*, 163–70, 174, 188, *190*, *197*, 200, 255

W

Wallower, 36, 76, 77, 83, 98, 282
Waltham, Mass., 167–68, 176, *264*
Washington, George, 36, *225*
Wassaic, N.Y., *85*, *268*
Water frame, 109
Water Mill, N.Y., 76, *268*
Water rights, 3, 9, 170
Waterman's mill (Chester, Vt.), *246*, 273
Waterpowered mills, 6–69, 130, 141, 241, 244, 249
Watertown, Mass., 28
Waterwheels. *See* Wheels
Watt, James, 108
Wauregan, Conn., *149*, *260*
Weather vanes, *80*, *145*, *160*
Wells, George Washington, 231
West Brewster, Mass., *41*, *264*
West Yarmouth, Mass., *44*, *264*
Westbeth (New York City), *257*, 269
Westbury, N.Y., *82*, *268*
Weston, Vt., *62*, 244, *272*
Wheels, 11–21, 36, *45*, *49*, 100, *101*, 218, 250, 282
  brake, 76, 77, 275

  breast, 11, *13*, *14*, 275
  face, 36, 98, *98*, 276
  float (paddle), 16, *19*, 277
  flutter, 16, 58, *65*, 250, 277
  horizontal, 11, 278
  overshot, 11, *12*, *13*, 29, *49*, 58, 95, *95*, *96*, 176, 183, *241*, *245*, 279
  pitch-back, 16, *18*, 176, 187, 279
  tide, 16, 281
  tub, 19–21, 64, *65*, 250, 281
  undershot, 15, *15*, 282
  vertical, 11, 36
White, Canvass, 197
White Rock, R.I., 141, *142*, *270*
Whitin family, 113, *119*, *120*, *140*, *145*, 164
Whitin Machine Works (Whitinsville, Mass.), 113, *144*, *145*, *189*, 265
Whitinsville, Mass., 113, *119*, *120*, 136, 141, *144*, *145*, 164, *264*
Whitney, Eli, 111
Wilkinson, David, 111, 112, 197
Willcox, Thomas, 224
Williams, Jeremiah, *46*
Willimantic, Conn., *147*, *149*, *260*
Wilton, N.H., *68*, *266*
Windmills, 64, 70, *71*, 72, *72*, *73*, *75*, 76, *76*, 77, *79*, 80, 81, *81*, *82*, 83, 239, 241, *242*, *243*, 265, 269
Wingdale, N.Y., *245*
Winthrop, John, 83
Woodruff, Robert, *67*
Woodruff family, 249, 261
Wool, 205–13. *See also* Carding mills; Fulling mills; Woolen mills; Worsted mills
Woolen mills, 102, *122*, 135, *136*, 137, 141, *143*, 157, 160, *162*, 206, 207, 210, *210*, *211*, *213*, 257, 265, 267
Woonsocket, R.I., 130, *132*, *134*, *135*, *270*
Worsted mills, *122*, 136, 271
Wright gristmill (Old Sturbridge Village, Mass.), *34*, *42*, 265

Y

York, Maine, 58
Young Millwright and Miller's Guide, The (Evans), 6, 38, *65*